Bible Study That Works

Revised Edition

David L. Thompson

Evangel Publishing House
2000 Evangel Way - P.O. Box 189
Nappanee, Indiana 46550

Cover design: Weston Phipps

ISBN: 0-916035-61-1

Printed in the United States of America

6   5   4   3

To my
Mother and Father
at whose knees I first learned
to love and live God's Word

Foreword

Listen to the words of Psalm 119. "I have laid thy word upon my heart, that I might not sin against thee" (v. 11). "I will delight in thy statutes; I will not forget thy word"(v. 16). "Give me understanding, that I may keep thy law and observe it with my whole heart" (v. 34). "...I find my delight in thy commandments, which I love. I revere thy commandments...and I will meditate on thy statutes" (vs. 47-48). "I will never forget thy precepts; for by them thou hast given me life" (v. 93). "Oh, how I love thy law! It is my meditation all the day" (v. 97). "Thy word is a lamp unto my feet and a light to my path" (v. 105).

What wonderful thoughts about God's Word these are! The burning question is: "Do we really live by these words?" James Smart has said, "The voice of the Scriptures is falling silent in the consciousness of Christian people, a silence that is perceptible even among those who are most insistent upon their devotion to the Scriptures."

The only antidote to this "strange silence" is to return to the thoughtful and careful reading of the Scriptures, and to become doers of the Word as well as hearers.

No one can do this for you. You must learn to do it for yourself. There is no substitute for individual, firsthand study of the Scriptures.

Your reaction might be, "But I don't know how! I have no special training." This book was written to help you to learn how to study the Bible for yourself, whoever you are. It is possible! It is necessary if you are to affirm the beautiful words of Psalm 119.

Dr. David Thompson is eminently qualified to lead the reader step by step into a life-changing study of God's Word. He has been a pastor as well as a teacher. He has dealt with people of varying backgrounds and abilities. He has been successful in leading people into the kind of "Bible study that works." He is enthusiastic in his love for God's Word. The thoughts of Psalm 119 describe his experience, and they can describe yours if you use this book conscientiously and prayerfully. You too will meditate on God's Word, understand God's Word, and find a more abundant life through God's Word.

> Robert A. Traina
> Professor Emeritus of Biblical Studies
> Asbury Theological Seminary
> Wilmore, Kentucky

Preface

Lay people and clergy alike exhibit a growing appetite for serious study of the Bible. This groundswell of interest in the direct study of the Bible has, in recent years, called forth a number of popular presentations of inductive Bible study to lead nonspecialists beyond superficial reading of the Word of God.

Like several of the other nontechnical works on Bible study method, *Bible Study That Works* owes an obvious debt at many points to the writing and teaching of Dr. Robert A. Traina, Professor Emeritus of English Bible at Asbury Theological Seminary and current dean of inductive Bible study in the vernacular in North America. In 1966 Dr. Traina came to Asbury Theological Seminary from an extraordinary teaching career at The Biblical Seminary in New York, and served at Asbury with distinction until his retirement in 1988. His excellent work, *Methodical Bible Study*, cited for further study in several chapters here, has influenced both the content and outline of this work in obvious ways.

In addition to Robert A. Traina, I must also express my profound debt to George Allen Turner. In the fall of 1962, in his course on the Gospel of John at Asbury Theological Seminary, he captured me for the sort of Bible study described in this work. To both Dr. Traina and Dr. Turner, my beloved teachers and esteemed colleagues, I gladly acknowledge my debt and express my joy in their continuing inspiration and instruction in my study of the Scripture.

This modest contribution to the ministry of presenting sound Bible study method in nontechnical language grew out of a series of articles which appeared in *The Wesleyan Advocate* in 1977. It aimed originally to encourage more adequate use of Scripture by lay persons and by clergy with inadequate preparation in biblical interpretation. As use of *Bible Study That Works* has continued, its readership has become clearer. Although few lay persons adopt the "whole program," many have found enduring help from the new orientation to Scripture learned from *Bible Study That Works* as well as from various specific pointers acquired. Pastors and Christian education directors have used the work not only for their own benefit but also as a point of reference for leadership training programs and church renewal efforts. Surprisingly, *Bible Study That Works* has proved useful as an introductory college and seminary text used in general education and Christian education courses and in other settings where a quick overview of an approach to be elaborated more technically over the course of a semester is sought. These various readers have been especially in mind as the revision has progressed.

It is my happy privilege to express my appreciation to Dr. George E. Failing, editor of *The Wesleyan Advocate* at the time of original articles' publication, both for his cooperation in the use of those articles which appear here in revised and expanded form, and also for the example of his own clear-minded study of the Scriptures. I am grateful as well to many readers who have taken time to write helpful suggestions for a revision of *Bible Study That Works*, and particularly to Carol Streeter and Linda Gail Adams who read the revised manuscript with an editorial eagle eye. Remaining shortcomings certainly cannot be laid at their door.

Finally, thanks to my colleague, Dr. Harold Burgess, whose friendly urging to put the *Advocate* articles in wider circulation led to *Bible Study That Works*, and whose encouragement supported this revised edition as well.

David L. Thompson
Asbury Theological Seminary
Wilmore, Kentucky

Contents

Chapter 1

Step Into the "Inductive Bible Study" Stream

In North America a virtual "inductive Bible study movement" exists. Its encouragement of serious study of Scripture in the vernacular (the reader's native language) has often led to this approach to Bible study being known as "English Bible," or just "EB" to devotees. Significant parts of this movement can be traced to the genius of Wilbert Webster White (1863-1944), founder of The Biblical Seminary in New York.[1] A product of traditional theological education in the 1880s, Dr. White became convinced of the utter inadequacy of that education at two points with regard to the Bible. First, he concurred with William Rainey Harper, the great Hebraist and later founding president of the University of Chicago, that theological students spent far too much time studying *about* the Bible and not nearly enough time studying the Bible itself. Second, White objected to the negative, fragmenting approach of critical biblical studies as it was carried on in the heyday of "higher criticism." He judged this approach incapable of sustaining Christian ministry and devotion.

White's experience as a student and assistant of Harper's at Yale introduced him to inductive study as a premier

---

[1]See Charles Richard Eberhardt, *The Bible in the Making of Ministers* (New York: Association Press, 1949), for the story of Dr. White and The Biblical Seminary in New York.

11

method of both learning and teaching. ("Inductive" study is an approach to inquiry in which students learn by examining the objects of the study themselves and drawing their own conclusions about these materials from that direct encounter with them.) Ministry and missionary experience in Illinois, India, and England convinced him of the power of Scripture studied directly and inductively to validate its own claims, and confirmed as well his confidence in the power of God to transform human character through it.

These convictions led Dr. White in 1900 to found The Bible Teachers College, later to be called The Biblical Seminary in New York. The school featured a curriculum centered in the direct study of Scripture in the vernacular and emphasized the inductive study of books of the Bible as literary, compositional units. This latter emphasis accented (1) the direct, independent study of the Bible, (2) the study of biblical books as unified literary compositions, i.e., "book studies," (3) the discernment of the literary and rhetorical structure of biblical books and their subunits as a means to discovering their meaning, (4) the drawing of interpretive and doctrinal conclusions inductively from specific data observed in the biblical text, and (5) the making of original and creative charts (of books and units) as a distinctive tool for analysis, synthesis and presentation.

These methodological distinctives thrived at The Biblical Seminary in New York for more than half a century. Developed and supplemented in various ways, they were carried by graduates, students, and teachers from the seminary to a host of schools, including major centers of theological education in North America, and were promoted through their writings. For example, among many others, Edward P. Blair[2] went eventually to Seattle Pacific College (now University) and then on to Garrett Biblical Institute (later Garrett-Evan-

---

[2]Author of *The Bible and You* (Nashville: Abingdon, 1953).

STEP INTO THE "INDUCTIVE BIBLE STUDY" STREAM   13

gelical Seminary). Joseph M. Gettys[3] went to The Assembly's Training School and on to the Presbyterian College (SC). Howard T. Kuist[4] went to Union Theological Seminary in Virginia and then to Princeton Theological Seminary, and Donald G. Miller[5] also to Union in Virginia and later to Pittsburgh Xenia Theological Seminary. George Allen Turner[6] and later Robert A. Traina went to Asbury Theological Seminary in Kentucky. Irving L. Jensen[7] went to William Jennings Bryant University; Oletta Wald,[8] to teach at the Lutheran Bible Institutes, first in Minneapolis, Minnesota, and later in Seattle, Washington. Through all these great teachers and their writings, thousands of students, both lay persons and clergy, have imbibed the passion for inductive Scripture study in the vernacular.

Hosts of others have benefited through parachurch organizations from the teaching and writing ministries of persons influenced directly by the "English Bible" movement. One thinks of Marilyn Kunz and Catherine Schell and their Neighborhood Bible Study ministry and literature, of Inter-Varsity's *Life Guide Bible Study* series and its successors, and

---

[3]Author of *How to Enjoy Studying the Bible* (Richmond: John Knox Press, 1946) and numerous works on "How to Study..." and "How to Teach..." various biblical books.

[4]Renowned for his stellar teaching and his writings, including perhaps his best known, *These Words Upon Thy Heart* (Richmond: John Knox Press, 1947).

[5]Author of *Fire in Thy Mouth* (Nashville: Abingdon, 1954) and other widely appreciated works in Scripture study and preaching.

[6]Author of *Portals to Books of the Bible* (Wilmore, KY: Asbury Seminary Press, 1972).

[7]Author of *Independent Bible Study* (Chicago: Moody Press, 1992 [first published, 1963]), and perhaps the most prolific producer of materials for inductive study of Bible books.

[8]Widely known for her little work, *The Joy of Discovery* (revised edition; Minneapolis: Bible Banner Press, 1956). In 1975 it was revised and divided into two works, *The Joy of Discovery* and *The Joy of Teaching Discovery Bible Study*.

of The Navigators, their devotional literature and the Nav-Press *Life Change* series and its successors. Less directly influenced efforts such as the Bible Study Fellowship International and Precept Ministries have also engaged multitudes in significant, direct study of Scripture. Several of these efforts flourish because of the ecumenical spirit inherent in the invitation to approach Scripture directly, asking only for a sincere desire to learn. With the rise of Vatican II and the increased emphasis in the Catholic Church on open Scripture study in the vernacular, the possibilities for fostering Scripture study among persons once divided by dogmatic boundaries have only increased.

In addition, some of White's progeny were pioneers in establishing constructive interaction between "EB" and traditional exegetical study on the one hand, and more recent critical methods focusing on the form and editorial or compositional history of biblical books on the other. Their insistence on understanding biblical books-as-wholes as meaningful literary compositions and on producing "results" edifying to the Church and the world made them people ahead of their time in the guild of biblical scholarship.

This constructive interaction was possible largely because W. W. White and his students created no radically new approach to Scripture that lacked significant ties with the church's historic study of the Word. Rather they offered a corrective, calling the church to reclaim important facits of its heritage. As we have seen, in place of the fragmenting tendencies in professional biblical studies, they called for understanding biblical books finally as meaningful, literary wholes, no matter how much one might learn of their compositional histories. In the face of the stifling effects of Scripture study captured by the need to vindicate already-held doctrinal convictions, they insisted on actually formulating doctrine *from* the study of Scripture, not the reverse. These emphases placed them in continuity with a stream of biblical study reaching back through the great fifteenth and sixteenth century reformers Calvin and Luther to such early scholars as Jerome (340?-420 A.D.) and the Antiochan fathers of the late second and third centuries and reaching out to the best in contemporary biblical scholarship.

With these brief notes the story is just begun. But this is enough to catch something of the breadth and depth of the stream into which we step in *Bible Study That Works*.

Chapter 2

Get the Basics Straight

Four questions demand an answer before any hints on Bible study can be considered. First, *"What* is Bible study?" Second, *"Why* study the Bible?" Third, *"Which* Bible should I study?" and fourth, *"What* are the basic questions?"

What is Bible Study?

To answer the first question, let's start with what Bible study is *not*. Bible study is not Bible memorization or Bible reading alone, though these exercises are beneficial in their own right and find a place in Scripture study. Neither is Bible study carrying, quoting, believing, or defending the Bible. Surprisingly, Bible study is not even a line-by-line comment or a verse-by-verse "sharing" on the Bible, whether done by a pastor or teacher, by a group, or by a solitary saint. Bible study of the sort envisioned in this work is the regular, careful, systematic *examination* of the Scriptures themselves, with an alert mind and a prayerful, open heart, and with the intent to understand and live God's Word.

In spite of the fact that *Bible Study That Works* will proceed with this target in mind, some important qualifications are in order. For one thing, not all persons wanting to study the Bible are believers, either in the God of the Bible or in Jesus of Nazareth as God's Son. Such persons may find talk of "a prayerful, open heart" and of "the intent...to live God's Word" odd or even distasteful. They may take courage in the fact that much of what will be said about Bible study in the following pages would prove equally understandable and useful to nonbelievers and to persons of faith alike. This is true because one does not have to believe a document to understand it at significant levels, even though some nuances of a text may well escape those who do not share the writer's own faith and world view. Still, if faith were a prerequisite to meaningful Scripture study, the Bible would be useless in evangelism, in bringing persons to faith.

"Regular, careful, systematic examination." These words may scare readers who have done little study of anything written or who are just beginning to approach the Bible seriously. They will be even more foreboding to persons who read little or have difficulty reading. So, do not read "technical, scholarly, microscopic, 'Ph.D.-ish' examination." The principles of Bible study and related methods presented in simple terms here can be used at any level of precision of which the student is capable. Beginning students need not apologize for starting simply and slowly, and more experienced interpreters should not feel constrained by the simplicity of the presentation. If you have difficulty reading the newspaper or popular periodicals, do not be surprised to find Scripture study challenging to you at the level of reading itself. Be kind and patient to yourself. You will be learning not only to study but also to read! What better book to learn with than the Bible.

So worthwhile Bible study is really study and requires effort, but its pace and scope are almost infinitely adaptable. Our situations, abilities, schedules, and opportunities vary widely. *Bible Study That Works* anticipates a lifetime of study with no single program or regimen for carrying that out. The approach outlined is well within the reach of any person of average abilities.

That Bible study is the study of *the Bible* would appear self-evident, but a survey of the numerous "Bible study" booklets purchased avidly by contemporary Christians of varying persuasions quickly shows the opposite. In spite of all the effort and good intentions currently focused on "Bible study," the amount of actual study of the Bible being done is surprisingly small. Too many "Bible study" booklets engage the student in question and answer exercises that require one-word or two-word answers. At best such "study guides" lead the student to selected biblical information on given topics. At worst they market the study guide's configuration of the selected information as "*the* biblical view" on topics ranging from economics to marital relationships. They never do lead to a comprehension of biblical books or passages as units, penned to real people at specific times to meet specific needs. They do not foster a grasp of the great biblical themes and their profound, practical implications for contemporary life.

Our intent, of course, is not to reject a sincere approach to God's Word by a variety of means. It is to point out that very few Bible study aids currently available lead students to more than a superficial grasp of the Bible. Even fewer give sincere seekers methods by which they can independently and intelligently probe the Word *for themselves!*

In addition, it is well to remember that the study of devotional books and the reading of Christian literature (even commentaries and Bible dictionaries!), though certainly recommended, is simply not Bible study, for which there is no substitute in Christian growth. Bible study is the study of the *Bible!*

Why Study the Bible?

The second question must also be answered: "*Why* study the Bible?" One answer is that because of its place as the greatest book in world literature, because of its massive influence on the history and literature of the world, East and West, one must study the Bible if he or she would be an educated person.

But more important for every Christian, one must study the Bible because of the crucial role of God's written Word in evangelism and Christian nurture. Scripture is one of the Holy Spirit's primary tools—if not the primary tool—for renovation of character and development of Christian conscience. To be sure, God uses significant persons and life in Christian community to this end (as Paul teaches in Eph. 4:1-16). And significant, personal encounter with the Living God substantially redirects persons (e.g., Acts 9 and 10). Even so, contrary to the notion perpetuated by some preaching and testimony, permanent, life-directing character change does not ordinarily come solely by a mystical sweep of God's Spirit through our being. Rather, as Jesus and the apostles clearly taught, we are changed within as we learn God's will by his Word, and we choose it as our way by his grace and Spirit. "Sanctify them by the truth," said Jesus. "Thy Word is truth" (John 17:17 NIV; compare also Eph. 4:20-23; Col. 3:16). The point in all of this is not to play the church or religious experience or the Bible over against one another, but to emphasize the important role of Scripture study in Christian nurture.

If one would "walk as Jesus walked," as John encouraged (1 John 2:6), how will one know, as a matter of fact, how Jesus did walk among people? How did Jesus treat women? What was his attitude toward religious tradition? What did he think was important in worship? What principles governed his actions? There is only one place where a sure and enduring answer is to be found—the Bible! If we would be like Jesus, we must learn his way through the Word and then by his grace choose it daily.

Closely related is the Bible's role in developing Christian conscience. One might think that, having given one's life to Christ, the Christian would almost intuitively know right from wrong in the world. But this is not so. On the contrary, if there is anything stressed by the apostle Paul, it is that the things often judged to be signs of piety and deep spirituality by good people are precisely the litter with which the path *away* from faith and grace is strewn (see especially Gal.

3, Col. 2, and Rom. 14). Left to ourselves we seem incurably inept at constructing true piety. God's idea of right is disclosed in the person of Jesus and the way of faith in him. This idea of how God chose to accomplish salvation for his creatures, "God's right way" (Rom. 3:21-22), must instruct our conscience. The textbook, again, is the Bible.

For this reason, the first step in Bible study for the Christian is really *prayer*—prayer that the same Spirit who inspired the writers of God's Word may inspire and illuminate our minds as we study, prayer for a humble and teachable mind. Although it will not often be mentioned hereafter, this first step in Bible study is the context in which all the rest of it takes place.

Why study the Bible—independently, regularly, directly? If I would know Christ's way and grow in it, there is little choice.

Astute readers will have noticed that *Bible Study That Works* uses the expressions "God's Word," "The Word of God," "The Bible" and "Scripture" interchangeably. This use does not aim simplistically to equate God's Word with the Bible or to restrict the Word of God to the Bible. It intends rather to echo the biblical writers' own apparent confidence that in the Scriptures they held dear, God himself spoke (e.g., Rom. 3:2 regarding the Hebrew Scriptures).

Furthermore, persons who looked up some of the texts just cited regarding the role of God's or Christ's "Word" in the development of Christian character and conscience (e.g., John 17:17; Col. 3:16) will have noticed that in these texts "word" does not necessarily refer to a written word, and certainly not to the Bible as we have it. The Gospel of John, for example, presents "the word of God" as a multifaceted concept. It encompasses at least the historic revelation to Israel (John 6:45; 8:35), the Father's communication with the Son (14:24), and the word of Jesus Messiah spoken on behalf of God (17:14). "The Word" even designates the Son of God himself, become flesh (1:14). Most likely it is the Father's word, spoken through Jesus, which is said to make holy those for whom Jesus prays (John 17:17). "The word of Christ" in Colossians 3:16 refers perhaps to the revelation of God in Christ or to the proclamation about Christ or tradition about Christ's own teaching—it is not entirely clear. In any case, this "word of Christ," lodging in the believers' hearts, forms part of the life-transforming resources and habits to which Paul points his readers (Col. 3:12-17).

While not confining the idea of God's Word to a written text, God's people early on experienced certain texts as veritably the Word of God to them, God himself speaking to them. Psalms 1, 19, and 119, among others, celebrate this conviction of the revelation of God in "The Law," God's "Torah" or "divine teaching." This confidence eventually extended to include not simply the Mosaic law but the entire Hebrew Scriptures (Christian Old Testament) and eventually for Christians the writings called the New Testament as well. Thus, the teaching, directing, transforming, enabling power of God's Word experienced more generally proved to be present in his written Word as well. For this reason, we invite careful study of the Bible.

It is fascinating that God's Word present in the biblical texts was never exclusively identified with any specific language form of the text. Thus New Testament writers already quoted as God's inspired Word various translations and versions of the Old Testament texts available to them. The early church did the same, using as the authoritative, written Word of God a widely popular Greek translation (the Septuagint) for its teaching and preaching during the early centuries of this era, and then for centuries using Jerome's Latin translation, called the Vulgate. At the same time, scholarly study of the Scriptures for the church relied increasingly on the biblical languages themselves, Hebrew and Aramaic for the Old Testament, Greek for the New Testament, setting up something of a tension. On the one hand, the church has come to base scholarly research for faith and practice on the study of

Scripture in the biblical languages. On the other hand, it has never renounced the confidence that God speaks his Word in all faithful versions of these historic texts in the vernacular. This leads to the question of which Bible you should use.

Which Bible Should I Study?

"Which Bible should I study?" or "Does God use 'thees' and 'thous?'" Discussion of Bible study method naturally raises this question. We offer the following guidance rather than a simple answer. First, study a Bible *in your own dialect*, because the whole point of the Bible is communication. For a variety of reasons some students may think they should use a Bible with older language forms, for example, "thees" and "thous," that seem on the surface to indicate respect for God and sacred things. This is understandable, but unless you regularly communicate in fourteenth English, you should seriously question advice to *restrict* your Bible study to any of the pre-nineteenth century versions. Rather, one should use several versions, including respected older ones, but also encompassing good translations in modern English closest to the language you use.

Second, use one of the standard (i.e., less idiomatic or non-paraphrasing) versions as a *basis* for careful, detailed study. Then, for increased insight, compare this basic study text with several others both new and old, paraphrasing and not. It is rarely a question here of choosing between "good" and "bad" translations. It is rather a matter of selecting a text appropriate to the use you intend.

All translations are interpretive to some degree; none can or should be completely literal. All good versions, which includes all those listed below and many more, intend to make the thought of the original text clear and understandable in the language of the target reader. They differ chiefly in the degree to which the translators choose to replicate the formal features of the original language such as grammar, syntax, and vocabulary in the process of translating the thought. More literal or "formally equivalent" versions seek to preserve as much of the grammar, syntax, and vocabulary of the original as the target language and good communication in it will permit. More idiomatic or "dynamically equivalent" translations focus on conveying the thought of the original, without regard for preserving formal features of the original text.

The *New King James Version* (NKJV), the American Standard Version (ASV, as the 1901 *Standard American Edition* of the British *Revised Version* was called), the *New American Standard Bible* (NASB), the *Revised Standard Version* (RSV), and the *New Revised Standard Version* (NRSV) are all examples of standard translations, as are the older *King James Version* (KJV) and *Douay-Rheims* translation (DR). The *New International Version* (NIV) stands close to them, though more influenced by dynamic equivalent translation theory. For careful, detailed study they are preferable to the more idiomatic or paraphrasing ones. They facilitate the discernment of themes and support more accurate tracing of thought between units. They also allow the vernacular reader limited but helpful access to rhetorical aspects of the original text, those artistic uses of language by which writers enhance communication.

More idiomatic or paraphrased renderings are excellent for rapid reading, for general survey, or for use as commentaries of sorts. But they are less suitable for detailed study. *The Message, The Living Bible, The Amplified Bible, Today's English Version* (TEV) or *Good News, The New English Bible* (NEB) and its successor, *The Revised English Bible* (REB), and Phillips' translations are among the most popular modern paraphrases and idiomatic or "dynamic equivalent" translations. *The New American Bible* (NAB) and *The Jerusalem Bible* (JB), along with its successor, *The New Jerusalem Bible* (NJB), stand somewhere in between these two groups of texts but toward the idiomatic side, as far as their freedom in translation is concerned. We can visualize this array something like this:

Standard Formal Equivalence Translations			Dynamic Equivalence Translations		Paraphrasing Translations	
NASB	KJV	NIV	JB	NEB	TEV	LB
	DR		NJB	REB		Phillips
	NKJV		NAB			Message
	ASV					
	RSV					
	NRSV					

A review of Romans 8:5-9 in several translations illustrates why one should not make a paraphrase or a more idiomatic translation the basis of careful study. In Romans 8:6 *Today's English Version* reads "To have your mind controlled by human nature results in death; to have your mind controlled by the Spirit results in life and peace," using the language of "control" as elsewhere in the context. In this case the NIV introduces the same concept: "...the mind controlled by the Spirit is life and peace," and similarly 8:9: "You, however are not controlled by the sinful nature but by the Spirit...." These renderings are perhaps suitable *unless* one is interested in the specific question as to whether or not one is, according to Paul, actually *controlled* by either a "lower nature" or by the Holy Spirit. Here the more interpretive treatment will give a premature answer, if not an incorrect one. For contrary to what one often hears, in Paul's writings the fruit of the Spirit is not *Spirit*-control but *self*-control under the *leadership* of the Spirit (cf. Rom. 8:12-14 and Gal. 5:23, KJV or RSV). The standard versions give a more neutral, less interpretive translation here: "To set the mind on the flesh is death, but to set the mind on the Spirit is life and peace" (8:6, RSV), and similarly in 8:9 "But you are not in the flesh, you are in the Spirit." This leaves the question open for students of Scriptures themselves to decide.

Parenthetically, one must raise a caution with regard to the whole matter of the use of numerous English versions (plural!). Although diligent Bible students will consult several renderings of the texts they examine carefully, they should decide which standard version will be their base for study and make it their point of reference. They should memorize it, quote it, pass it on to their family and friends, and make it part of their very being. Only in this way can one overcome the most ironic hazard of the ready availability of numerous English versions, the tendency to read them all and memorize none.

But why should you study the Bible in your own dialect as opposed to older forms of English? There are three compelling reasons. We treat them briefly here, but expanded reflection upon them appears in chapter 7. First, study in your own dialect *to take seriously the pattern of biblical revelation itself.* This pattern reveals God's commitment to communicate. God spoke to people in varying cultures and in succeeding centuries in the language of their own day, not in previously canonized, "sacred languages." God inspired persons to address him in the same forms they used to talk to other intimate, contemporary friends, not in any special speech. We have no indication that this pattern has changed.

Secondly, you should include a modern English version at or near the center of your Bible study *to keep faith with the translation passion of the Church.* This passion reveals the saints' commitment to communicate. This "translation urge" of God's people to put his Word into the language and dialect of the contemporary readers has from the start produced an almost unending parade of revisions and translations, reaching back even before New Testament times. Surely such persistent and apparently edifying work has been born of the Spirit of God.

Finally, you should study the Scripture in your own tongue *to appropriate the power of God's Word in your own life.* Scripture should be *God's* communication with you. If you are to read God's Word with the immediate, contemporary, attention-demanding impact intended by the One who inspired it and supported by the church which transmitted it, you should study the Bible in your own language—not in the dialect of your ancestors. In your devotional and study habits as elsewhere in your religious exercises, you must resist like the plague any language or artificial roles that divorce piety and worship from daily life, from the home and market-place, and relegate them to "sacred" places, special times, and lingo known only to a privileged few. God does not use "thees" and "thous." Why should you?

What Are the Basic Questions?

Much of what one can learn in specific suggestions about Bible study can be summarized in two basic questions that are well worth memorizing. Answered thoroughly, these two questions give significant guidance to a student of the Word.

1. *Question number one: What, as a matter of fact, did the authors intend to say to their first readers?* This question takes several important matters into account. First, it leads the reader to recognize the *historical* nature of biblical revelation. The Bible was written over a particular span of history from the late bronze age to the Roman period (roughly 1500 B.C. to 100 A.D.). It was written to specific people, with their particular cultures, customs, and needs in mind. For example, 1 and 2 Kings are not simply an objective history of Israel preserved for antiquarian interest. Those accounts were penned for the disheartened, disillusioned Jews of the exile (cf. Ps. 132). They desperately needed an explanation from the Lord as to how the city of God and the temple could possibly have fallen, in view of the promises to David. (Remember 2 Sam. 7:8-16?) And Romans was written to imperial Rome, Corinthians to corrupt Corinth, and so on.

One must remember, then, that the Bible was written first to those specific readers, with the Holy Spirit knowing that we would be reading over their shoulder, so to speak. So—and this is tremendously important—if one wishes to avoid distorting the biblical message, one must begin by asking what the author intended those first readers to understand, not what is being said to us. That comes later.

Secondly, this question calls attention to the *objective* nature of the Bible. This claim does not intend to reduce Scripture to a "mere object" of study, something simply to be mastered by students. Indeed Scripture presents not only an object to be studied, but a subject which itself speaks to the reader with the voice of the living God. Neither does it raise hopes for naive "objectivity" whereby students, even if they wished to do so, could approach Scripture divorced from their own culture with its values and world view. The question rather acknowledges that the Bible stands independent of me. This collection of classic documents remains God's Word whether or not I see it, matters of record with which I must come to terms, which I neither created nor am free to modify.

So, the question leads directly to the first step in sound Bible study, "Look before you leap." *Look* at what the author actually wrote before you leap to interpret or apply. *See* what is really there. See the passage clearly. See its details in light of the whole. See it in light of its context. In subsequent chapters we will pursue this important matter of looking— what to look for, how to look. For now it is enough to get the sequence straight. One must see what the author said, all of it, and clearly, before moving to interpret or apply it.

Thirdly, the question concerns the *authors' intent*. Several facts complicate this aspect of our question. For example, numerous biblical books are anonymous. We do not know the author(s). Some works are of multiple authorship, involving composition by various persons over extended periods of time (e.g., the book of Proverbs, as indicated by Prov. 1:1; 10:1; 25:1; 30:1; 31:1). Furthermore, we know that authors cannot control what readers (either immediate or later readers) make of their writings, and that writings take on different meanings as they are read in different cultures and contexts. These and other factors complicate the business of inquiring after the "authors' intent."

In spite of the complex problems lurking in such a claim, the orientation to seeking the meaning intended by those who gave us the text is significant and worthwhile. Every text, including anonymous works, carries an author implied by the writing itself, one whose intent can be inferred at least in part from the writing. Even though one will no doubt never completely or perfectly apprehend the author's mind in a text, the quest still provides an orienting safeguard, much like a compass on a wilderness trek, directing readers initially away from their own world and values to the world and ideas of the text and its writer(s). Such an orientation is particularly appropriate to persons convinced that God's revelation in history includes or at least involves Scripture.

In addition, although it is true that readers *can* make whatever they will of a writing, they do not *have* to do so. And, although readers should not and indeed cannot divorce themselves from their own settings as they approach Scripture, they need not be hopelessly captured by their own culture. If this were true, cross cultural communication would not only be difficult, which it is, but impossible, which it is not. Instead, like open participants in a conversation with another person whose world and culture is foreign to them, readers can seek to listen actively to the Scripture texts on their own terms, and to understand insofar as possible what the authors intended to say. Readers can hope to set up a conversation across time and space even with ancient writers, a conversation in which the readers' own preconceptions and biases are increasingly unmasked and the meaning of the texts themselves becomes increasingly clear.

Finally, the question takes seriously the *authority* of the Scripture. Our question, "What, as a matter of fact, did the authors intend to say to their first readers?" does not at this point ask concerning what one's church says they said, what the Christian classics say they said, and what the preacher or evangelist say they said, what one's parents have said they said, or what one wishes they had said. Rather the question directs the student to take seriously the fact that the Christian disciple lives first under the lordship of Christ and his Word (Matt. 28:19-20; John 14:23-24; Phil. 2:9-11). This does not mean that one is preoccupied with finding discrepancies between the Bible and one's church and its documents, between the Bible and the preacher, one's heritage, or even one's own ideas. Nor does it mean that good Bible study is done in isolation, ignoring the church's historic interpretation of the Word (more on this later). But it surely does mean that Christ and his Word remain to this day judge of all the earth—including your church with all its personnel and publications, and including your backgrounds and preferences. If that is not true, claims about believing the Bible or receiving the Bible as one's "standard for faith and practice" are ridiculous if not blasphemous.

When Christian witness, devotional literature, even well-intentioned counsel or preaching are not seriously evaluated by the Word, frustration and confusion in faith and practice arise. The common understanding, for instance, that anger has no place in the life of the Christian well illustrates that point. Now the Bible clearly insists that a life governed by anger and malice, characterized by inner storm and bitterness is incompatible with life in Christ (Col. 3:5-10; James 1:19-21). But it is equally clear that the apostles nowhere envision a person *incapable of anger* at any stage of piety as either possible or desirable. They rather point one to Christ as the model in all things, presumably including our anger (Eph. 4:1-16, 20-21). In Scripture one sees Jesus capable of intense anger (e.g., Mark 3:1-6) but governed by redeeming love (Mark 10:45; Eph. 5:1-2).

So it is that Paul's explicit command is not that one never be angry, but rather that one experience anger in such a way and for such reasons as not to lead to sin. "Be angry, but stop sinning [in the process]" (Eph. 4:26). "Don't nurse your anger overnight" (Eph. 4:26). Make sure you have a better reason for anger than your own personal inconvenience or mistreatment (1 Cor. 6:1-8). But for heaven's sake, don't stand in the presence of real injustice or misrepresentation of the truth with a conscience so limp that it remains unstirred (cf. Mark 10:13-14; 11:15-19).

"What, as a matter of fact, did the authors intend to say to their first readers?" Thus, the first question begins the process of Bible study with *observation*, seeing what the authors actually said, and with *interpretation*, seeking to understand what they meant.

2. *Question number two: What does that have to do with us and our world?* This question calls attention to at least two important items which can only be mentioned now and left for more extended comment in subsequent chapters. First, it leads one to consider the fact that not all of the Scripture relates to us in the same way. Put positively, it acknowledges that different Scripture passages inform contemporary Christian readers in different ways. This is not a question of the relative importance of various parts of the Bible nor a denial that all Scripture has relevance for contemporary readers. It is an inescapable question of just how specific passages of the Bible come to bear upon our lives now. As we shall see, this is in the end a question of assessing the conversation that goes on *within* the Bible on various topics.

Second, it insists that one cannot be content with a purely academic study of the Word, always learning and never coming to a knowledge of the truth and its powerful significance for every age, including our own. So the second question moves on from observation and interpretation to evaluation and application. The question should perhaps even imply that one has in most cases not fully understood until one has acted in response to Scripture. It is enough now to remember that the Lord of the Scripture will not be content until in some considerable way his Word "becomes flesh" in us (James 1:22-25).

For more extended treatment of these matters consult Robert A. Traina, *Methodical Bible Study* (New York: Ganas & Harris, 1952; reprint, Grand Rapids: Zondervan, 1985), pp. v-26. Recurring reference will be made to this fine text at the end of several chapters. Robert Traina's *Methodical Bible Study* is a college or seminary text, but is within the grasp of lay persons accustomed to stiff reading and to analytical thought.

Chapter 3

Look Before You Leap

Suppose you want to answer that first basic question, "What, as a matter of fact, did the authors intend to say to their first readers?" Begin by looking carefully at what they wrote. Look at what the author said before you leap to interpret and apply! So, assuming a context of prayer, the first step in good Bible study is *observation*. And one must see two things. First, one must see what is there; a matter of the *contents*. What is the book or unit at hand actually about: sin or grace, prayer or faith, Abraham or David, creation or second coming? These are matters of content, of observing what was said. Second, one must see how what is there is put together; this is a matter of *structure*. How is the material arranged and how are the thoughts tied together? So one begins by seeing what is there and how it goes together.

Study in Units

Study in units—few disciplines will revolutionize your Bible study more than this. The reason is obvious. When you read the Bible in this way, you begin to see through the eyes of the author. Most, if not all, of the biblical books were penned finally as units, regardless of the history of various sources used by the writers and regardless of the complex paths by which various biblical units came to their final, canonical "edition." It was assumed that the unit had significance as a whole and that every section would be understood in light of that whole.

Reading the book of Jonah, for example, one will ponder the implications of Jonah's flight from God in chapter 1. But the insights will be limited at best unless the reflection takes seriously into account the *last* chapter of the book. There Jonah gives the reason for his "escape" from God in the first place—a deep-seated disagreement with God's mercy, if it included the hated Ninevites too (4:2ff.). His disobedience and running from God were far more than quibbling over a call. He had a basic argument with God. Only one who sees the book as a whole will uncover that, and yet it is a main point of the book.

Aim at seeing books as wholes. Begin to see chapters as collections of related paragraphs whose main points form an intelligent whole. Give attention to individual verses only as you can see them in light of the paragraph and chapter in which they are set. Start this discipline now!

Use an edition of the Bible printed in paragraph units rather than one that sets each verse apart as a unit standing on its own, a misleading "verse paragraph." If you have never attempted the study of the Bible by larger units, for practical reasons begin with a more basic book (Mark or Galatians before Esther or Ecclesiastes) and a smaller book (Mark or Colossians before Acts or Revelation), or simply a section of a book.

Studying in units makes use of different "study lenses" in sequence. First, the *wide-angle* lens to get the big picture (survey). Second, the *close-up* lens to look carefully at the parts that compose the larger picture (analysis). And last, the wide-angle again to see the unit as a panorama once more (synthesis), now with greater perception after detailed exposure to the parts. We will give attention here to the first phase, since that aspect of Bible study is rarely used by non-professionals and holds such promise for enhancing your understanding of Scripture.

See What is There: The Content

The following suggestions are useful in seeing what is actually in the unit selected for study and in beginning to see that unit as a whole.

1. *Survey the unit.* Read the book or set of chapters through quickly to get an overview. You will have to work at this if your pace has been verse by verse. Read the unit this way (several times, if possible), observing persons, places, and themes of overall importance. Note these (pen and paper!) for further study.

2. *Title chapters, paragraphs and other subunits.* On one of these survey readings, give short, descriptive titles to each paragraph and to each "chapter."[9] If you see several chapters which seem to go together to form larger units, give titles to these units as well. In shorter books, one can name the paragraphs, chapters, larger units and the book itself and still keep the whole in mind. But in longer books—perhaps more than five or six chapters—naming each paragraph can lead one to lose the forest in the process of naming the trees. Think, for example, of naming all the paragraphs in Isaiah's sixty-six chapters in an "overview" reading! Obviously, these judgments are not matters of right or wrong, but of what proves most helpful for the student. Experience is the best teacher here.

Use imagination and don't underestimate the value of this exercise. Short, information packed titles (three to five words) are best. Make them memorable, so they serve as

---

[9]Chapter and verse numberings are editorial notes to make reference more convenient. Chapter divisions often roughly coincide with thought divisions. Thus students may want to begin by simply taking the chapters as tentative divisions and naming them. But your reading may indicate places where you think the thought unit comprises a collection of paragraphs slightly larger or smaller than the standard chapters. Such discernment may mean you are at a stage where you could well name these "segments" in place of the chapters. The same could be said for paragraph division.

reminders of the unit's contents. And don't worry about what someone else might think of them. The task here is to put the essence of the unit's *content*, whatever its size—paragraph, segment, section, division, book—in the title. As such, titles which describe the content with as little interpretation as possible serve best. More interpretative titles will be useful later. These titles put handles on an entire book or unit in an amazing way. Try it!

3. *Note proportion and sense the atmosphere.* Without getting bogged down in detail, note how much space is devoted to each item in your unit. Stick with major features here. In Jonah, for example, one would note the surprising amount of space devoted to the prophet's attitude problem—one entire chapter in four! And one would sense the shift from Jonah's helpless tone in chapter 2 to the sullen, argumentative mood of chapter 4. What a change of atmosphere!

4. *Observe the literary type and genre.* Is the book or unit written in prose or poetry (or both)? Most modern translations set poetry off with indented lines to help you spot this shift. The kind of literature in a particular part of Scripture is called *genre*. Our understanding of genre enables us to know how a writer intends his or her work to be understood. For example, a parable is to be taken differently than an international treaty, a business letter differently than a love letter. So note whether the passage being studied is a narrative of history or events, a letter, a legal code, a prophecy, a song, a prayer, or an essay. It will make a difference in how you interpret its materials.

5. Make *a chart and draw a picture.* Present your survey findings regarding the content of the book or other unit in chart form, incorporating your unit titles (paragraphs, chapters and other units) and any other survey information you can in such ways as to show their placement, relative size and other interaction. Here are two examples:

Jonah: Running from God's Mercy (Book as a whole)			
Jonah runs from God	Jonah prays from the fish	Nineveh repents, God relents	Jonah angry at God's mercy
1:1 16	1:17 2:10	3:1 10	4:1 11

Mark 2:1–3:6 Questions for the Son of Man (Segment as a whole)				
Who can forgive sins?	Why eat with sinners?	Why not fast?	Why not on the Sabbath?	To heal or to harm?
2:1 12	13 17	18 22	23 28	3:1 6

Relevant information about time, place, main persons, etc., can be conveniently placed beneath the appropriate section title on a chart like this.

So much for seeing what is there and doing so in units. We must turn now to the second feature of the observation process, seeing the structure.

Look For the Design: The Relationships

A story can be told in any number of ways. How it is put together is a matter of design—in the Bible, inspired design. The fact that a given biblical unit begins proceeds and ends as it does, develops the themes, poses the questions and answers, presents the causes, effects, climaxes, contrasts, and comparisons that it does, is all a matter of design. At times this design appears by the deliberate choice of the inspired writer, sometimes simply as the result of spontaneous or intuitive thought. In any case the discovery of that design (the literary structure) is the reader's task. Its study returns lavish dividends.

That the biblical authors structured their writings with design arising out of their respective purposes is obvious in the gospel writers' presentations of Jesus. The four evangelists begin the story four different ways: Matthew with a genealogy (a list of ancestors) and infancy narrative through Joseph's eyes; Mark with the ministry of John and Jesus' baptism (without reference to the birth of either); Luke with the conception of John and Jesus and the latter's youth; and John with a prologue introducing Jesus as the eternal, divine Word become flesh. John plainly says he selected (and apparently also arranged) his materials according to an overall purpose (John 20:30-31; cf. Luke 1:1-4). These differences, then, are a matter of inspired choice, not literary chance. The more students see this and study it, the more they think the writer's thoughts after him. Try the following suggestions in your Bible study and watch yourself leave superficial reading behind!

1. *Learn the basic structural relationships.* Discovering the design (the structure) of a biblical unit is simply seeing how its various parts fit together. One's skill in perceiving how an author has put his work together can be greatly increased by learning the basic relationships used by writers in structuring their compositions. The following concepts should become stock-in-trade study tools for the serious Bible student, for they are standard literary tools of all authors, including those inspired by the Holy Spirit. You will see that we are here simply labeling the standard ways human beings link ideas together. Start by learning the following relationships; discern others as you gain experience in study.

a. *Cause-effect relationships.* When A produces B, or A results in B, or A leads to B, they stand in a cause-effect relationship. Thus in John 3:16 God's love is the cause; sending the Son is the effect or the result of that love. In that same context, belief and unbelief are contrasting causes, each having their own contrasting effects—eternal life, on the one hand, perishing and condemnation on the other. Linking words and phrases like "therefore," "then," "so then," "consequently," and "as a result" express this relationship.

Sometimes the effect precedes, followed by the cause as in Romans 1:16: "I am not ashamed of the Good News about Christ [the effect], because it is God's power unto salvation to every person who believes" [the cause]. Connecting words like "for," "because," and "since" are clues here. Cause→effect is called "causation" and expresses results; effect←cause is called "substantiation" and expresses reasons.

b. *Climax.* A series of elements developing a theme in a crescendo of feeling, importance, or intensity to a final high point of that theme forms a climax. So Hosea's work begins with the major comparison depicting God's love in Hosea's parable marriage (Hos. 1-3). But then again in chapter 6 (The Dilemma of God's Love) and chapter 11 (The History of God's Love) the subject of Yahweh's love reappears, moving with increasing urgency to the climactic, unexpected Invitation of Love in the closing chapter (Hos. 14). This book of judgment is designed to end in a climax of divine love. Think of it! And think of how differently the book of Hosea would read if it were designed to end at 13:16, even if the love invitation and prayer of confession in chapter 14 were included somewhere in the preceding sections, say in chapter 11. Can you find the climax in the book of Jonah and identify the themes that build to that climax?

c. *Comparison.* Here one item is laid beside another to illustrate or illuminate it by calling attention to similarities between the two: A ≈ B. Often "like" or "as" are used. In Psalm 103:13 the Lord's pity for those who fear him is illuminated by comparison to a father's attitude toward his children—that's the sort of heart God has. The major comparison of the harlot, Gomer, to Israel, and the loving Hosea to God in Hosea 1-3, has been noted already. What important comparison do you recall from the Lord's Prayer (Matt. 6:12)?

d. *Contrast.* Here opposite items are set side by side: A ≠ B or A vs. B. What contrasts do you see in John 3:16? In Romans 6:23? Jonah 4 is structured by a basic contrast throughout. Two opposing sets of attitudes are carefully put side by side by the author. What are they, and what do they involve? Pursue it; you'll be amazed. "But" and "however" are the common clue words here.

e. *Cruciality (the pivot).* A passage that takes a major turn, reversing a previous course, is said to be structured by cruciality. Pivot names a particularly striking contrast that turns at a specific point. 2 Samuel is so designed, with the turning point set clearly in 11:27b. Pow! *To* that point the writer presents the rise of David's house, *from* that point its decline, and *at* that point the crux of the reversal—David's sin with Bathsheba and specifically God's attitude toward it: "But the thing that David had done displeased the Lord" (2 Sam. 11:27b, RSV). One can usually see causes producing the drastic contrasts involved here.

f. *General-specific* relationships. When the author moves from a specific statement to a more general saying on the same subject, he *generalizes.* Doing the reverse, moving from a general *to* a more specific statement, one *particularizes.* The design is called "particularization." Matthew 5:17-48 is structured by particularization. Jesus' general statements about fulfilling the law (5:17) and about righteousness exceeding that of the scribes and Pharisees (5:20) are followed by six more specific examples of how this fulfillment and true righteousness are to be understood (5:21-26, 27-30, 31-32, 33-37, 38-42, and 43-48). Several psalms, like Psalm 103 or 148, begin with a general exhortation to "praise" or "bless" the Lord, particularized, i.e., detailed by the presentation of specific features of this praise in the psalm, and then conclude with another general exhortation similar to that with which it began (generalization). What particulars follow and expound the general statement in Matthew 6:1? Find them and relate them to 6:1. Sometimes generalization-particularization is used to describe focus or scope. The movement in the Gospel of John from more public and geographically wide-ranging interaction between Jesus, the Jews, the people, and disciples in general in chapters 1-12 to the narrower focus on Jesus and the twelve around the table in a specific setting in chapters 13-17 would be an example.

g. *Introduction.* Passages which prepare the way for the presentation that follows are introductory. These orientations provide context by introducing characters, setting, ideas, and other information in light of which the following materials will be read. Thus, the dramatic cycle of speeches in Job is introduced by chapters 1and 2 which emphasize the wealth and piety of Job and the origin of his ills in his goodness rather than in any sin. These introductory paragraphs provide this and other information known only to the reader and the writer (not to Job and his friends) and in light of which the speeches have particular meaning.

h. *Question-answer (problem-solution).* Many biblical passages are structured by the presentation of a question with its answer(s) or a problem with its solution(s). "Interrogation" designates this structure. The book of Exodus is designed this way. Problems are presented in chapter 1-5 to which the plagues, the exodus, the covenant, and the tabernacle are God's solutions. Romans 6 presents two questions, 6:1 and 16a, with their answers 6:2-14 and 16b-23. Look at Mark 7 and Matthew 24 in this way and see what you find.

i. *Recurrence.* Recurrence is the reappearance of words, phrases, ideas, themes, structures, or other elements, whether the same or slightly altered. Recurrence is used to develop emphases and themes in a unit and is one of the most common tools used to structure biblical materials. See how the writer of Amos used recurrence to tie the prophet's indictments against Israel's neighbors together effectively as an introduction, while zeroing in on Israel in Amos 1:3-2:8.

Other structures could be mentioned and these could be analyzed and illustrated further. But these provide tools for a good start.

2. *Find the design.* Knowing that authors use the sorts of relationships listed above to tie their materials together, read the Bible looking for them. Read with structure in mind, whether your unit is large or small. These relationships are most easily discerned between small units like phrases, clauses, or paragraphs. But aim also to see those structures that bind large amounts of material together, such as the contrast running throughout the whole of Jonah 4, or the problem-solution design that unites the whole of Exodus. The writer put the material together in the way he felt was most effective. Don't miss it! Look until you think you see what the design was.

Remember the cruciality by which 2 Samuel is structured (see e, above)? There is no particular reason why the writer could not have introduced the entire story of David's royal family with an observation in chapter 1 that its destiny hinged largely on the "royal affair" with Bathsheba. But he did not. Instead, there is not the slightest hint that this event, objectively recounted in chapter 11, spells disaster for the king. After all, kings can do as they please, can they not? But then one comes to those closing lines of 2 Sam. 11: *God's* assessment of King David's conduct would prove critical to his future. That fact must be observed to catch the real punch of the book. Look for structure!

Thoughtful persons often raise questions at two points if they have never before given deliberate attention to the structure of biblical materials. First, they wonder if they may be imposing Western, overly analytical categories on Scripture. Second, they wonder if the biblical writers really were aware of using "causation," for example, and thus if the search for such structures is not an imposition on the Word. Both of these questions are reasonable, but neither need deter us. First, one can rest assured we are here describing *human* thought patterns, not Western or Eastern structures, or ancient or modern ways. Review of documents from the various cultures of the ancient and modern world, East and West, shows the same thought patterns.

Second, with regard to the level of intent with which writers "chose" to structure their thoughts, perhaps our own experience at this specific point can help. Of course neither we nor presumably the biblical writers think of labeling our thoughts as "causation" or "substantiation." We do know the experience of planning how we will write a letter, phrase a paragraph, close a speech, and the like. We know that when we speak and write, we do so in structured ways, whether deliberately or not. We also have the experience of moving without trouble from "normal," intuitive speaking or writing, in which our thoughts have simply been structured by habits of communication, in a split second to more intentional structuring, where we actually choose a given conjunction or word order, deliberately designing how our words will appear. The student's task is to see the text as it *is* structured, no matter what level of intention produced it.

3. *Probe relationships.* Don't stop with the *observation* of an author's literary design. Go on to probe these relationships with questions focusing both on the structure itself and on the specific materials as arranged by the writer. In Matthew 5, for example, one must not stop with the discovery that most of the chapter is built around the specific statements growing out of Jesus' more general sayings on fulfilling the law, and on righteousness exceeding that of the scribes and the Pharisees (particularization). One must press on to ask questions: What do the general statements about fulfilling the law and righteousness exceeding that of the scribes and Pharisees really mean? What do each of the related particularizations mean—being angry with the brother and saying "you fool" (5:22), looking lustfully (5:28), divorce and unchastity (5:32), not swearing at all (5:34), not resisting evil (5:39), and loving your enemies (5:44)? What did Jesus and

Matthew really intend by each of these? Why were these general statements the first major focus after the introduction to this address as Matthew records it? Why are they expounded by these particular examples? How does each of the more specific paragraphs give meaning to the concepts of fulfilling the law and righteousness beyond that of the scribes and Pharisees? What does all this imply?

These are sample questions to which you can find answers if you study the passage, gather relevant information, and reflect prayerfully on it. The point is this: when you have seen something in the Bible (here a relationship), don't leave it there. Press on to probe it for meaning, using questions to be answered by further study. More will be said on this in the next chapter; however, for now, get started looking for what the author said and how it goes together in the Bible unit you have chosen to study.

For further study read Traina, *Methodical Bible Study*, 31-88.

Chapter 4

Ask Questions and Find Answers

Asking questions is the bridge that joins seeing what the author said (observation) and understanding what he meant (interpretation). This interpretive process is so important that it merits separate attention as a major step in Bible study that works.

Understanding written documents resembles meaningful participation in a conversation. Two persons in a conversation understand each other "intuitively" or "naturally," one might say, provided the language used is well known to them both. They speak and listen with understanding, without really thinking about the understanding process itself. They use their mental data bank, with its vast dictionary of terms and its complex understanding of grammar and other information from their shared culture. The more "actively" these persons listen to each other, the more intentionally they try to hear correctly, the more fully they share each other's culture and enter empathetically into the other person's situation, the more adequate this initial, "intuitive" understanding will be. Few participants, even from the same family, would claim to understand each other perfectly in most conversations. Thus, their intuitive understanding, though adequate in some ways, will be partial. It may even be incorrect at points. Even so, this immediate, intuitive grasp provides a starting place for growth in understanding.

But what if the conversationalists wish to go beyond this level of understanding? Perhaps they know even as they speak that they are missing something, or perhaps they wish to understand more adequately or confirm their understanding. Then the process of understanding itself becomes intentional. They will need to ask questions and get additional information.

So also when we read texts like the Bible in our native tongue or in languages well known to us, we have an immediate, intuitive understanding of the text. Without conscious effort we use our mental data bank, with its vast dictionary of terms and its complex understanding of grammar and other information from our culture and beyond. The more "actively" we "listen" to the text, the more intentionally we try to read accurately, the more fully we share the writer's culture and enter empathetically into the text's situation, the more adequate our initial grasp will be. The less we know about the world of the biblical writers and readers and the less aware we are of the differences between our own world and theirs, the less adequate our "intuitive" understanding of the Bible will be, and the more likely we will be to read our religion and culture into the biblical text.

Just as with intentional conversation, we can go beyond this immediate, intuitive grasp of the text to a more intentional, reflective understanding. We can move from partial, at some points incorrect and inadequate understanding to a more complete, more adequate grasp of what the writer actually intended to say to his first readers. We do this by asking questions of what we have read and then finding information to answer those questions.

Learn Standard Questions to Get at Meaning

Most persons know about the questions Who? What? Where? When? Why? and How? but do not exploit their full potential in Bible study. Wise Bible students will learn the *set types of questions* which need to be asked and will address them to every major matter they observe in the text. They will give attention as well to the sort of information they seek through the questions.

The most important standard questions are the following:

1. Ask questions to get *definition:* Who or what is this? What does this [term, phrase, sentence, item] mean? What is involved in this [term, phrase, sentence, item]? What is the significance of this?

2. Ask questions to learn *reasons:* Why is this so? What is the purpose?

3. Ask questions to understand the *means:* How is this done?

4. Explore *implications* and assumptions with questions: What is implied by this? What does this assume?

5. Ask the other questions regarding place and time as they are appropriate.

Don't assume too readily that you know what the text means. Observing that Jesus said one must be "born again" to "see the Kingdom of God" (John 3:3) is one thing; knowing what Jesus meant is another. Of course we know, or think we do, what modern evangelists mean by being "born again"; we know what current pamphlets mean by the phrase. But what did Jesus mean by it in the first century A.D., being a Jew and talking to a Jew who had never heard "accepting Christ as Savior" or "becoming a Christian" or other expressions now associated with the phrase in some sectors of the church?

Don't allow these and other questions to float distractingly around in your mind. Rather, write them down for reference, rephrasing them to get at the specific materials you are studying. Record as many questions as you can from as many different angles as possible on a specific passage. Just the asking sharpens your perception of the depth and breadth of a passage. The answers will give you the meaning.

Question Major Matters First

Attend to major matters first and to details only as they relate to the whole. Here is where the previous observation of the unit as a whole and of its inspired design can be of great help. This will generally mean focusing questions first on the materials as you have seen them to be structured, guided by your understanding of the unit's structure. For if you see how the author put together a whole unit and then focus your questions on the materials most important to that design, you will not become bogged down in chasing peripheral matters. Rather you will pursue matters of overall importance to the unit's meaning and the author's own emphasis.

Focus questions first on material involved in important structures. For example, if you observe that Jonah 4 presents throughout the whole chapter a major contrast between Jonah's attitude and God's, don't let the matter drop there. Proceed to explore that discovery with your "tool kit" of standard questions. Then look for answers as you are able. Work right through the various types of questions you should ask. Address questions of *definition* to this insight concerning the contrast: What are the aspects of Jonah's attitude and of God's which are set forth here? What is involved in each? What is the meaning of each of the major terms used in the presentation, e.g., Jonah's anger and God's compassion and pity? How do they differ from one another? What is the basic, deep-down contrast?

Ask for reasons guided by the structure: Why does the writer present this contrast? Why present it here at the end of the book? Why does Jonah's attitude differ so completely from God's? Why does God pursue the question of Jonah's anger? Why in the manner chosen?

Because the "why question" lends itself so readily to undisciplined speculation and to ad hoc proposals without foundation in the text itself, a caution is in order. We ask the why question not to launch such unfounded speculation, but rather, to seek answers in the text itself. We will answer it, like all the others, on the basis of evidence. We will discover the need to proceed with caution, even with evidence. For the reasons why certain things appear in the text, why the writers wrote and actors acted as they did, will often be difficult if not impossible to discern with certainty.

Ask for implications guided by the structure: What does the contrast in attitides here imply? What does the author assume about Jonah's motives? About God's? What is implied by the fact that the book ends with this contrast? What is implied about the nature of obedience? About the nature of God and his will for his people? About the value of persons? About the sin of bigotry and the gravity of selfishness by this stark contrast?

Or again, when you see that Mark 2:1-3:6 is designed to bring together a series of important questions addressed to Jesus on major aspects of his person and work, don't drop the matter there. Go on to pursue this question-answer structure with adaptations of your standard questions, and you will rapidly get beneath the surface of this unit.

So, guided by your structural observations, ask for *definitions:* In each of these paragraphs, what really is the main question posed, and what really is the answer given to each? What is the meaning of the most significant words in the main questions and in their answers?

Address questions about *reasons* regarding this collection of questions-answers: Why were these questions asked about Jesus' person, his deeds? Why did Jesus answer in each case as he did? Why are these questions and answers brought together in this way for the reader? Why are they placed here at the outset of Mark's presentation of Jesus?

Ask regarding *manner:* How does each answer reply to the question asked?

Ask for *implications:* What is implied by each of these questions and answers? Implied about the writer's concerns? About the people's understanding of Jesus? About Jesus' understanding of himself as presented by the writer? What is implied about the nature of worship? About the meaning of keeping the law? About the import of the Sabbath for Jesus' disciples?

Do you see the pattern? Don't get side-tracked at the beginning in discussing the architecture of the tiled roof in 2:1-12 or the precise type of grain in 2:18-26. They will be important as you do more detailed study. The questions and the answers were apparently the author's main concern. So focus your attention there, pursuing other details at this point only insofar as they contribute to your grasp of these central matters. Then ask whatever other questions you wish when you have finished dealing with the main concerns of the passage.

In addition to the stock set of questions which every interpreter of the Word should have ready to ask at a moment's notice, there is also something of an order to follow in both asking and in answering the questions. Like other matters of Bible study, this order should not rigidly confine creative work. Instead, it should serve as a guide to proper interpretation. The order: first definition; then reasons, means, implications, and other questions. The reason is obvious. One cannot well reflect on why something is, or what it implies, until one knows what it is. To return to John 3, one cannot say very well why Jesus said one must be "born again" or what is implied by it unless one knows what the phrase actually means. Begin with the definition, the who and what questions.

Find Answers

Bible students often ask questions but then either simply make up answers based on their past experience or immediately consult an expert's opinion in a commentary, a Bible encyclopedia or Bible dictionary. "*Find* answers!" this section encourages. And do so mainly or at least first in the Bible itself. Just as we have sought to discover what is actually in

the Bible by examining it directly, so we aim at interpreting
it (i.e., answering questions we have about it) by drawing
conclusions from information gathered from the text itself.
The help of others will prove important as well, and to these
resources we will return. But first we focus on the primary
resources available to all Bible students for finding answers
to their questions. Most of these resources reside in the text
and its setting and are not under the control of the interpreter. Others are within the interpreter or his or her
observed or shared experience. All are important.[10]

1. *Context—its content and flow.* Many important questions can be satisfactorily answered from the content and
flow of context—the immediate context or the larger context
of the whole book or related passages in other biblical books.
That is why this section says, "*Find* answers!" They are there.

For instance, when you study Mark 3:29 on Jesus' statement about "blasphemy against the Holy Spirit" and "an
eternal sin" which "never has forgiveness," the place to look
first for a definition of what "blasphemy" might mean is in
the immediate context. There the attitudes and conduct of the
persons referred to by Jesus are clearly shown (Mark 3:19b-
27).

The persons involved were well acquainted with the
Hebrew Scriptures and had apparently come from Jerusalem
for the very purpose of observing Jesus. They had evidently
seen his works and knew his claims. They categorically
rejected Jesus and his teaching as having anything to do
with God and good. He is of the devil, they said. There was
far more at issue here than a few words passed between
them and Jesus, merely a so-called "taking the Holy Spirit's

---

[10]The following discussion owes considerable debt in its outline to
Robert Traina's discussion of "Determinants of Interpretive Answers,"
Methodical Bible Study, 135-165. Dr. Traina's distinction between "subjective determinants" (spiritual sense, common sense, and experience) and
"objective determinants" and his recognition of the validity and importance of the so-called "subjective determinants" is particularly helpful.

name in vain." A whole mind-set (review Mark 2:1-3:6) and way of life was expressed in their derision of Jesus. That, implied Jesus, could be blasphemy against the Holy Spirit, which would never be forgiven. The answer from the context is more illuminating than one you will dream up by mere reflection on preaching or testimony, or looking in a Bible dictionary.

At the end of this same chapter (Mark 3) Jesus says that "whoever does the will of God" is his true relative. One will certainly ask what he meant by "the will of God" (definition). What does one do who lives God's will? Go to the context. Start with that series of questions and answers in Mark 2:1-3:6. There God's will as reflected in his Son was stated on four major issues of life in the Kingdom of God. There you will find God's will on forgiveness (2:1-12), on ministry by association (2:13-17), on the place of religious observance in the disciples' life (2:18-22), and on the priority of compassionate action over legalistic observance of law (2:23-3:6). There from the context is an excellent start on the answer to your question. Or perhaps the immediate context in the paragraph itself is all that is necessary in this case to define "doing the will of the Father." We may observe what those to whom he referred (3:34) were doing—sitting and listening eagerly to his teaching. If so, those who "do the will of the Father" would be those who wish to know and understand his way, as opposed to the scribes in 3:21 ff., who have already rejected Jesus as an impostor. Eventually this should be related to other places in Mark where he specifically attends to the issue of the "will of God" (Mark 8:33; 14:36).

Not only the content but also the flow or logic of the context provide valuable information to build answers to our questions. Consider 1 Corinthians 2:9 (KJV): "Eye hath not seen, nor ear heard, neither have entered into the heart of man, the things which God hath prepared for them that love him." The context shows that, contrary to much popular misunderstanding, the apostle is not here speaking of the unknown glories of the new heaven. The paragraphs around this text make it clear that Paul was quoting Isaiah 64:4 not to talk about what we do *not* know, but, on the contrary, to affirm what we *do* know.

The thought-flow is clear: (a) Paul preached at Corinth only the simple gospel of Christ crucified (vs. 1-5); (b) nevertheless, among more mature believers elsewhere he taught "a secret and hidden wisdom of God" (1 Cor. 2:6-7, RSV); (c) this wisdom was beyond the comprehension of the power people of this world (v. 8); (d) but, and here is the point of the famous quote, "What no eye has ever seen" *on its own*, "God *has revealed* to us through the Spirit" (v. 10; emphasis added)! Paul then proceeds to explain that the problem lay not in his inability to teach more than the basic gospel principles, nor in the Holy Spirit's ability to show mankind the deep mind of God, but rather in the Corinthians' own immaturity which prevented their grasp of more exalted instruction (2:11-3:4).

This text, then, is a statement about the amazing fact of God's ability to reveal himself and his will to us by his Spirit, and about the inability of people on their own to comprehend God's wisdom. And it arises in a discussion of the need for Christian maturity. The content and thought-flow of context is always the first and best place to find answers to one's questions.

2. *Major terms—their form and use.* Questions of definition and basic meaning will involve the identification and the understanding of the major terms or expressions of a unit. For example, discovering the meaning of the contrasted attitudes in Jonah 4 would surely involve an understanding of the terms "anger," "compassion," "pity" and particularly "relent/repent" which appear to be important to that passage.

Acceptable answers regarding the meaning of a word or expression must be drawn from its observed *form* in its context. Thus, for instance, Paul's statement in Ephesians 2:8 must include the meaning of *accomplished, present* salvation.

The statement reads: "By grace you *are* saved through faith." While Paul elsewhare talks of the ongoing process of salvation (e.g., 1 Cor. 1:18) and of the future completion of God's saving work (e.g., Rom. 8:18-25), here Paul asserts that the Ephesian Christians are *now* in some sense saved. The English expression, "are saved," is present perfect, describing a present condition, a fine translation of the Greek perfect which here lies behind it. The interpreter's understanding is determined by the form/inflection of the words in the expression (present perfect, not future, not past or present continuing).

Furthermore, the context here in Ephesians 2 is consistent with Paul's use of the word elsewhere, leading to the conclusion that "saved" must here have to do with a *gracious rescue* from the personal and social consequences of sin, a transfer from death in sin to life in Christ, out of alienation from God to fellowship with God and his people. "Saved" does not mean merely to be "forgiven," or to be "acquitted" or "loved." The use of the word here and elsewhere simply will not allow such weakening, but rather points in a different direction.

Discovering the meaning of a word or expression means studying its *use* as well. Bible words, like our own, are best defined by their use, not by a simple "dictionary definition." Here we extend "context" study, for studying a word's use means discerning its meaning based on the other contexts in which it is found as well as the immediate context where one has first encountered it. One investigates each of its occurrences saying, in effect, "If all I knew about this word or expression were its use here, I would think it meant _____, " or, "Judging by its use here, this word or expression means _____."

Definitions of words can of course be found in Bible dictionaries and encyclopedias, but Bible students will often be better served to do their own study of the words. In order to study the use of a biblical word, two pieces of information are necessary: 1) the biblical references where the word appears, and 2) the identification of the Greek, Hebrew, or Aramaic term translated by the word you are studying. The biblical references are necessary, of course, simply to find the other occurrences of the word. Identifying the Greek or Hebrew word guarantees that one is studying a single word and not different words which happen to be translated by the same English term.

For example, in the Authorized Version (KJV) of the New Testament the English word "perfect" translates three different Greek words, which have only superficial relationship to each other and are distinctly different words, from different backgrounds, with different emphases. Thus, the student studying 2 Timothy 3:17, "That the man of God may be *perfect*, thoroughly furnished unto every good work," (KJV, emphasis added) will be misinformed if he or she relates this use directly to the set of occurrences where "the perfect" are contrasted with immature persons as in 1 Corinthians 2:6; and Ephesians 4:13 ff. where a second Greek word is used, or to Luke 1:3 where still a third word underlies the translation "perfect." The word translated "perfect" in 2 Timothy 3:17 has to do with fitness, preparedness, being equipped for a job. The second word used by Paul or others has to do with being grown up (usually in Christ and defined by love). The third word, used by the historian Luke, has to do with accuracy. None of these words is related to the others. While some more recent versions will help the student avoid confusion in these particular instances, the problem is inherent in translation and will arise no matter what version one uses. Examples could be multiplied almost endlessly.

But resources are available which allow the student both to locate the places where the word under study appears and to avoid confusion with other similarly translated words. These resources are of two types: analytical concordances and so-called "Englishman's" concordances. Analytical concordances list by reference the occurrences of words in the translation language (e.g., English), using some system (usually numbers) to distinguish various biblical language terms being translated by the same word. "Englishman's" concordances list by reference the occurrences of biblical language words in translation, and then provide some system by which those who do not read Greek, Hebrew, and Aramaic can locate a specific term. The following are recommended:

Goodrick, Edward W. and John R. Kohlenberger III, (eds.). *The NIV Exhaustive Concordance*. Grand Rapids: Zondervan, 1990. (NIV)

Kohlenberger, John R. III, Edward W. Goodrick, and James A. Swanson (eds.). *The Greek-English Concordance of the New Testament*. Grand Rapids: Zondervan, 1993.

Strong, James. *The New Strong's Exhaustive Concordance of the Bible*. Reprint. Nashville: Thomas Nelson, 1990. (KJV)

Thomas, Robert L., (ed.). *The New American Standard Exhaustive Concordance of the Bible*. Nashville: Holman Bible Publishers, 1981. (NASB)

Wigram, George V. and Jay P. Green, Sr. *The New Englishman's Greek Concordance and Lexicon*. Peabody, MA: Hendrickson, 1992. For the New Testament.

Wigram, George V. *The New Englishman's Hebrew Concordance*. Peabody, MA: Hendrickson, 1992. For the Old Testament.

Young, Robert. *Young's Analytical Concordance of the Bible*. Reprint. Peabody, MA: Hendrickson, 1984. (KJV)

The use of each work is explained in its introduction. A half-hour spent learning to use any of these tools is time well invested.

Finding a word that appears scores or hundreds of times can discourage students from doing their own inquiry. In such cases, when an exhaustive study is not possible, one will do well to limit inquiry to literature by the same author (say to Paul's letters if you first encountered your word in Romans), or to the same type of literature (say to the gospels if you are studying a word from Matthew, or to the prophets, if you encountered the word first in Jeremiah).

Also, even students without a knowledge of biblical languages have access to the Hebrew and Greek language lexicons (dictionaries) for the Old and New Testaments respectively. Recent editions of classic (though at some points now out of date) lexicons are keyed to Strong's concordance. Thus, having located a word from the Old Testament in Strong, one could follow its number to locate the treatment of the Hebrew word involved in the Hebrew dictionary by Brown, Driver, and Briggs. At first sight the Greek and Hebrew scripts on these pages will seem intimidating. But with a bit of patience, English-only readers will find much information helpful to them and learn to screen out the rest. The lexicons can be particularly helpful in laying out quickly the range of meaning exhibited by a particular word and some of the references in which those meanings appear.

In addition, more technical works treating the meaning of important Greek, Hebrew, and Aramaic terms can be surprisingly intelligible to and useful for the non-specialist. Of these so-called "wordbooks," the two best resources currently available for students without biblical language mastery are:

> Brown, Collin, ed. *The New International Dictionary of New Testament Theology*. 3 vols. Grand Rapids: Zondervan, 1975-1979.

> Harris, R. L.; G. L. Archer; and Bruce K. Waltke, eds. *Theological Dictionary of the Old Testament*. 2 vols. Chicago: Moody, 1980.

The Old Testament resource (Harris) is keyed to Strong's concordance, and the New Testament work (Brown) is arranged topically. This means that persons who know neither Hebrew nor Greek can locate the biblical language terms they want to study. Both resources spell the Greek, Hebrew and Aramaic of the biblical language terms with characters of the English alphabet (i.e., they "transliterate" them), and thus make their work accessible to non-specialists.

A second major resource, then, for building answers to one's questions is in the form and use of major words and expressions of a unit.

3. *Author's intent.* The significance of a passage must agree with the author's intent, as best it can be determined. Thus John says, "By this we know love, that he laid down his life for us; and we ought to lay down our lives for the brethren. But if any one has the world's goods and sees his brother in need, yet closes his heart against him, how does God's love abide in him?" (1 John 3:16-17, RSV). John's statement enjoins love *between* members of the Christian community ("brethren") and does not expressly address love beyond this circle. While this is true, to use this statement as a basis for *confining* Christian love to fellow members of the Christian community would be a terrible misreading of the spirit of the apostle and a misuse of his writing. Elsewhere in this work John stresses the universal reach of Christ's redeeming life and death (1 John 2:2) and God's example of loving us before we love him (1 John 4:10 and 19). Surely this indicates a stance which makes it difficult to conclude that John intended love to be calculating or confined in any way. To cite another, more obvious example in this letter, interpretation of John's statements regarding sin and its confession must take into account his clear statement of purpose in 2:1: "My little children, I am writing this to you so that you may not sin" (RSV).

Sometimes the author's intent is not clearly stated and must be inferred from the content of the document under consideration. At other times, "authorship" may involve a complex process, entailing the use of resources by a series of editors (as clearly in the book of Proverbs and the Psalter and no doubt many other places in Scripture as well). In these cases, we assume someone finally put the document we now have before us together with intention and purpose. This purpose we seek to discern. As elsewhere, we try to allow the evidence to speak for itself and to refrain from firm conclusions when the evidence will not allow it.

4. *Historical setting*. Discovering the meaning of biblical terms and expressions sometimes requires historical and cultural information which will not surface simply in a study of the word's use. It is a constant temptation to forget that the cultural setting of the biblical writers differed significantly from ours. We tend to think first of our own customs and to assume those referred to in the Bible were similar, when they were in fact often quite different. The expression "sinners and tax collectors" in Mark 2:16 (RSV) is a case in point. Mark records that the scribes of the Pharisees asked why Jesus ate with such persons. In order to understand the question, one must know that the Pharisees classified all persons who did not keep Pharisaic tradition as "sinners," not just particularly wicked persons or persons who disobeyed the law of Moses. One must also know something of the graft and corruption almost inherent in the system of tax collection under which the revenue agents of both Herod and Rome worked. Thinking of them simply as ancient IRS agents, working within the limits of modern tax codes, will lead one astray. Tax collectors were universally assumed to be "on the take" and ranked with thieves and murderers in Jewish tradition. The boldness of Jesus' lifestyle and the force of the Pharisees' question emerge clearly with such information.

Two major approaches to gathering information about the historical setting of Scripture commend themselves, one general and one specific. Serious students of the Bible often come to make general reading in the history and culture of the biblical world an agenda of lifelong learning. Over the years they read books and articles enhancing their grasp of those distant times and places. Texts specifically devoted to this endeavor and resources not primarily devoted to biblical studies, like *The National Geographic*, prove useful here.

Students also often find themselves looking for historical information related to the specific aspects of particular biblical texts they are studying. For these more focused, text-specific inquiries, Bible dictionaries and Bible encyclopedias prove most useful. The following works are examples of the excellent resources available to help the student find information on such matters:

> Achtemeier, Paul J., ed. *Harper's Bible Dictionary*. San Francisco: Harper & Row, 1985.
>
> Bromiley, Geoffrey W., ed. *International Standard Bible Encyclopedia*. Rev. ed. 4 vols. Grand Rapids: Eerdmans, 1979-1988.
>
> Buttrick, George Arthur, ed. *The Interpreter's Dictionary of the Bible*. 4 vols plus Supplementary Volume. Nashville: Abingdon, 1962, 1976.
>
> Douglas, J.D., ed. *The New Bible Dictionary*. Rev. by Norman Hillyer. Wheaton, IL: Tyndale House, 1982.
>
> Freedman, David Noel, ed. *The Anchor Bible Dictionary*. 6 vols. New York: Doubleday, 1992.
>
> Tenny, Merrill C., ed. *The Zondervan Pictoral Encyclopedia of the Bible*. 5 vols. Grand Rapids: Zondervan, 1975.

Commentaries will also bring relevant historical and cultural information to bear on specific texts (see "Other Interpreters."). Consult the bibliography at the end of the book for other resources specifically devoted to the historical, cultural background of the Bible.

5. *Other interpreters*. This work emphasizes skills by which Bible students can study and understand Scripture for themselves, directly and independently. But "independently" does not mean "arrogantly" or in isolation from the wisdom of others who have also sought to understand the Bible. Studying "by myself" *or* with the help of "secondary sources" presents a false choice. A better approach has Bible students first encountering the text for themselves, seeing

what is really there for themselves, and then drawing conclusions about its meaning from data found there, *and doing
so in conversation with other interpreters ancient and modern.*

There are less interpretive secondary sources (like a concordance or grammar) and more interpretive resources (like
Bible dictionaries and commentaries). All of them can help
the serious student when viewed as partners in discovery,
resources to assist one's own wrestling with the text. Consultation of a Bible dictionary to sharpen or correct our picture of a "tax collector" in first century Palestine is an example of the assistance such a partner can be. In almost every
case use of such resources will be enriched by one's own
preliminary study.

The following are examples of excellent, single volume
commentaries available:

> Brown, Raymond E., Joseph A. Fitzmyer, and Roland E.
> Murphy. *The New Jerome Biblical Commentary.* Engle-
> wood Cliffs, NJ: Prentice-Hall, 1990.
>
> Carpenter, Eugene and Wayne McCown. eds. *Asbury
> Bible Commentary.* Grand Rapids: Zondervan, 1992.
>
> Elwell, Walter A., ed. *Evangelical Commentary on the Bible.*
> Grand Rapids: Baker, 1989.
>
> Guthrie, Donald and James A. Motyer. eds. *The New Bible
> Commentary.* 3rd ed. London: InterVarsity, 1970.
>
> Laymon, Charles M., ed. *The Interpreter's One-Volume
> Commentary on the Bible.* Nashville: Abingdon, 1971.
>
> Mays, James Luther, ed. *Harper's Bible Commentary.* San
> Francisco: Harper & Row, 1988.

Multivolume commentaries are also available for more
extensive interpretive treatment of each passage. See the bibliography for excellent examples.

Almost all the types of Bible study resources and even
some of the specific resources mentioned in the four preceding sections are now available in a wide variety of computer software. These programs range all the way from relatively simple to very complex programs. At one end of the

market there are very focused, single function programs offering information of a specific type, for example, on Bible geography or providing text search capability of one or more versions. At the other end stand very powerful, highly integrated programs which bring together numerous resources and capabilities in a single program. These programs will often give immediate, integrated access to:

- English and foreign language versions of the Bible
- Biblical language texts
- Analytical concordances (mainly Strong's)
- "Englishman's" concordances
- Topical Bibles
- Commentaries
- Biblical language lexicons keyed to Strong's concordance
- Word books

and more. These programs include sophisticated capabilities for word and phrase search, including Boolean searches, for grammatical analysis and more.

Because these materials develop so rapidly, one hesitates to recommend specific products. Nevertheless, in order to give some indication as to the resources available, we list the following without version numbers as among the best multitask programs currently on the market:

AnyText. Linguist's Software. Edmonds, WA (DOS).

BibleSource. Zondervan. Grand Rapids, MI (DOS).

BibleWorks for Windows. Hermeneutika. Seattle, WA (DOS, Windows).

Logos Bible Software. Logos Research Systems, Inc. Oak Harbor, WA (DOS, Windows).

MacBible. Zondervan. Grand Rapids, MI (Mac).

OnLine Bible. OnLine Bible USA. Bronson, MI (DOS).

WORDsearch for Windows. NavPress Software. Colorado Springs, CO (DOS, Windows).

Some programs, like those of The Gramcord Institute (*GRAMCORD* for DOS and *acCordance* for Mac) are sufficiently technical that they will be most useful to the scholarly community. Some analysts think the future of Bible computing will be in CD Rom format. Dallas Theological Seminary's *CD Word Library* (now produced by Logos Research Systems) holds the field in that area at present, with other entries likely to follow.

Christian Computing Magazine, published by Christian Computing, Inc., Raymore, MO 64083, presents perhaps the best place to look for current information on programs available to assist in Scripture study. Feature articles, detailed descriptions of the latest programs, and ads from leading companies make it a handy source of up-to-date information. Leading religious periodicals also regularly contain special advertizing sections which include information on computer programs for Bible study (e.g., the *Bible Reference Update* insert in *Christianity Today*). Several companies publishing the printed resources referred to above also produce and/or market software for Bible study. Local bookstores can put catalogs from these companies in your hand, and can provide other information on software for Bible study. Some seminaries have media services, like the Multimedia Center of Asbury Theological Seminary, Wilmore, Kentucky, which one might call for information on these matters.

At its best, consultation with other interpreters transpires not only through the printed page and electronic media but also face to face in community. Consultation then becomes *conversation* among a group of informed interpreters. Enlightening one another, challenging and questioning one another, they move the group toward sound conclusions. Such conversations can involve informal work by a few or formal conversation by many; they may be brief or cover decades. This interaction proves so important that enduring conclusions regarding the meaning of Scripture are usually produced in group study of some sort.

So context, word form, word use, author's intent, historical setting, and other interpreters are sources of information external to the modern interpreter and beyond his or her control, even though their discovery and use involves judgment. Some other significant sources of information for interpretive answers are found within the interpreter's experience or that of other persons.

6. *Spiritual discernment.* This is a sense born not so much of age as of prolonged exposure to the Scripture and sincere, deepening association with the living Word himself. It is an ability to discern the "ring of truth" in an interpretation that goes beyond data and evidence to intuition born of the Spirit of God. This sense by God's Spirit, often best gained by converse in the Christian community, has safeguarded the mass of interpreters in the life of the church who, though untutored in technical biblical interpretation, have lived devoted to God through Christ. The resulting consensus of interpretation in the history of the church is amazing, the many different viewpoints notwithstanding.

7. *Common sense.* This source of information for answering one's questions calls the interpreter to stick to the most obvious meaning of a text and reject hidden or overly subtle meanings proposed. Deliberate exaggerations and figurative expressions are taken as such. Overly technical interpretations are excluded from material not intended for technical understanding, say in biology or botany (cf. Jesus' words about the "mustard seed," (Mark 4:31), allowing the biblical writers the freedom which we ourselves require to communicate.

8. *Experience.* The interpreter's own experience is not the final yardstick for determining Scripture's meaning. On the one hand, the fact that I have not yet witnessed a resurrection from the dead does not allow me either to deny the reality of such an occurrence or to redefine the word. At the same time, biblical interpretation must match life as we experience it. This should caution the interpreter against making Jesus' statement, "If you abide in me, and my words abide in you, ask whatever you will, and it shall be done for you" (John

15:7, RSV), an unqualified promise regarding positive answer to prayer. The experience of Jesus and the apostles, along with that of the devout of the church, leads to the conclusion that a qualification is implicit. In this case the test of experience should lead the student back to the context and to the text itself to a more careful consideration of qualifications actually present there.

So then, by looking carefully in the immediate and the larger context, by studying the use of significant terms both on one's own and with the help of secondary sources and the other sources of information considered here, answers to questions can be found. These sources of information are also tests of one's interpretive answers which can lead in the end to sound understandings of the Word of God.

Actual *lack of ability* will seldom thwart persons seeking to discover the meaning of Scripture. More often they will stumble over one of two opposing hurdles. On the one hand, some will ask many questions and then will assume they cannot find answers, since they are not specialists. They will fail to hear the Word significantly because they underestimate their own ability to see and understand, and because they fail to use resources available to help in the search for answers. On the other hand, others will fail to ask questions, naively assuming they already understand the Scripture. Or they will fail to look for answers, thinking they already have all the answers. They will substitute traditional, abbreviated, and often very distorted understandings of Scripture for an authentic Word based on personal inquiry and openness to the Spirit. Either mistake is a tragedy. Others—"and these are those who hear the Word"—will not only observe and ask questions, but will proceed to find answers. They will discover that Jesus spoke the truth: "The words that I have spoken to you are spirit and life" (John 6:63, RSV).

For further study read Traina, *Methodical Bible Study*, 89-200.

Chapter 5

Let Jesus Be the Judge

Just how the Bible is to be applied to the nuclear age is a topic of great debate. A chief obstacle to application is the sheer breadth of revelation in Scripture and the diversity arising in it. The Bible exhibits a dynamic and profound unity, but not a simple uniformity. As a result, persons are often surprised at the range of instruction given regarding a topic. They come to the Bible inquiring as to what they should think or do about item "a," and expecting a single, straight-forward answer. Instead they find that the Bible in various passages says "Do a1, a2, a3, a4" and so on. No matter how it is done, one must weigh the biblical passages related to the issue at hand, discerning how they relate to the issue and to each other to form a basis for thought or action. This reflection follows interpretation and precedes application.

All biblical interpreters, professional and lay, engage in this evaluation process whether they know it or not. No one lives directly by all the Bible's teachings at once. Its diversity prevents this. For example, one cannot simultaneously practice the sacrificial system of Leviticus and the approach to God taught in the book of Hebrews which sets aside that Levitical system. Simply to say that one must "take the Bible literally" as though one could somehow avoid making the difficult judgments involved in this process, will not do, for literalness is not the issue. In fact *meaning* is not the issue, for we are now asking how to *apply* passages whose meaning we have in some sense discovered. All of us therefore must be selective in the passages we take as mandates for our own lives. We must recognize this and attempt to be consistent, and more important, to be faithful to the intent of biblical revelation in our very ordering and selection.

When one speaks of evaluating biblical texts it is not a question of importance or unimportance, or inspiration or lack thereof, of any part of biblical revelation. Nor is it a question of relevance, for all Scripture relates in some way to readers of all ages. It is rather a question as to just how specific passages are to be related to our setting, at least nineteen centuries removed from the original writing and culture.

The following guidelines for evaluation arise from the nature of the biblical materials themselves. Though by no means exhaustive, they can help increase the consistency and perceptiveness with which one lives the Bible in today's world. The "guidelines" also present sources of information from which one can draw evaluative conclusions. Just as in seeking answers to our *interpretive questions,* we will seek here to answer our *evaluative questions* on the basis of evidence from Scripture itself. Often no single guideline, no single source of information will support our conclusions. Instead frequently several lines of evidence converge to lead us to sound conclusions in evaluation.

Keep the Sacred Story Straight

Remember that the Scripture was written over a period of at least twelve hundred years and probably much longer. During those centuries and many preceding ones described in the Bible, God patiently taught people of himself, of his ways, and of how they might live with him by faith. Pacing himself partly by his creatures' ability to understand the truth and partly by his agenda for their instruction, God nurtured them as a father would a child, as Hosea expressly says (Hos. 11:3). This is why the first "Sermon on the Mount" was the Mosaic law and not the discourse of Jesus on perfection in love (Matt. 5:44-48). This fact was well known to the New Testament writers (Heb. 1:1 ff.).

When one reads the Old Testament particularly, one must remember that the passage at hand may not have been God's last word on the subject. Subsequent biblical revelation may have refined, revised, or even rescinded the instruction one is now studying. One must consider this before setting out to "live the Word," transporting that word directly to the present century. As noted above, the Levitical laws of sacrifice and ceremony are obvious examples of passages whose direct application to present Christians would often be impossible and usually pointless. But there are other important instances of moral and spiritual teaching which are inadequate without reference to later instruction by the Father.

At this point, parenthetically, we remind ourselves that *all* Scripture is relevant to believers of all times and places. All Scripture is "useful," to use Paul's word (2 Tim. 3:16, NIV). Thus, even though Christian's do not apply the Levitical law *directly* in sacrificial and dietary practice, these texts inform us in many important ways, providing history, context, theology, and perspective without which we would be at a loss to understand much of the New Testament itself.

In order to keep the story of biblical revelation straight, one need not master all the details of Old and New Testament history. Begin by learning the major periods of biblical history—patriarchal, Mosaic, conquest, united monarchy, divided monarchy, exile, restoration, life of Christ, and apostolic period—and the centuries or decades covered by each. Any standard Bible dictionary or encyclopedia will provide summary articles on Old and New Testament history. Some study Bibles have excellent introductory essays on this subject. Study these and make your own chronological chart, noting major events and persons. Give particular attention to correlating prophetic and apostolic writings with their settings as presented in the historical writings of the testaments.

Kings and Acts respectively are important in this regard. For example, put Amos in the decadent, final decades of the Northern Kingdom and 1 Corinthians in the light of the setting given in Acts 18. Then think particularly in terms of the chronological placement of biblical documents, as opposed to biblical persons, for in the end it is the ordering of these documents that most influences the evaluative process.

Separate the Local from the Universal

Separate what is of local, historically limited significance (as far as application is concerned) from what is of universal significance by penetrating beneath the surface to the principle being addressed in each passage. Probe to the underlying issue with which passages deal. Observing how God instructed his people pertaining to the same or related issues in differing historical circumstances can help one separate the local from the universal.

Thus in the book of Exodus, God delivers his people "to himself" (Exod. 1-19; cf. especially 19:1-6) in order to offer them his covenant which they were to accept and keep in grateful response to their rescue from Egypt (Exod. 20-40). More than a thousand years later Paul reasons similarly with the Ephesian Christians. God has saved them by grace through faith (Eph. 2:1-9), in order to offer them the opportunity and the grace to "walk" in his ways (the "good works," Eph 2:10, expanded in chs. 4-6). Unlike Moses in the book of Exodus, Paul does not instruct the Ephesian Christians to keep the whole Torah of God. He rather directs them to grow up to the stature of Christ, to live the truth as they have learned it in Jesus, to be "imitators of God" as seen in Messiah's love, and to live full of the Spirit, relating to others in reverence for Messiah (Eph. 4:13-16, 21; 5:1-2, 18-21).

The specific content of the "will of God" by which the people of God at Ephesus are to live differs in many particulars from that given to the early Israelites at Mt. Sinai. But the same issues surface in both passages: the questions of the purpose of God's saving action and the nature of the response he anticipates from that rescue. Differences abound between Egypt and Ephesus, between slavery under Pharaoh and bondage to sin, between the Law of Moses and the "walk in love" in Christ. Still in both of these settings, so widely separated in time and culture, God rescues his people by grace through his mighty power in order that they may walk in his ways in grateful response to him. Seeing what changed and what stays unchanged in these passages provides evidence for discerning what was of relatively local significance, and what was applicable to other times and cultures.

To acquire some idea of the principles which are foundational in biblical faith, one should become conversant with those passages which, by the structure of the books or major sections therein and by the express statements of the authors involved, are treatments of God's highest will for humanity or are outlines of life in the kingdom. Such passages include Matthew 5-7, Romans 12-15, 1 Corinthians 13, Ephesians 4:1-16, Colossians 3:12ff., Philippians 2, and others. Let us consider this further.

Matthew 5-7 presents something of a "constitution of the Kingdom" for followers of Jesus. A narrative setting puts the unit before us as an authoritative teaching by Jesus— given on the mount, delivered from the seated position of a respected teacher, directed clearly to his disciples and perhaps to the crowds as well (5:1-2). We note first its introductory section, 5:3-16. In the form of "beatitudes," this introduction describes in general terms the people of the kingdom of God, persons blessed by God, in implicit contrast to persons rejected by God, (5:3-12). It then describes these persons as "salt of the earth" and "light of the world" (5:13-16). Through these persons the Father in heaven receives glory (5:16). Presumably such persons enter or are a part of the kingdom of heaven which Jesus claimed was at hand in his own coming (4:17). This introduction presents in general terms the qualities of kingdom life expounded in greater detail in the succeeding four units of the discourse (5:17-48; 6:1-18; 6:19-34; 7:1-23).

Moving to the conclusion of the discourse, Jesus claims that response to this teaching ("my words") determines human destiny. Those who hearken stand, and those who do not fall with great catastrophe (7:24-27). Surely the intervening instruction will be of critical import. For if 5:3-16 does indeed introduce the instruction and if 7:24-27 indeed concludes it, then the intervening materials will expound what it means to live under the blessing of God, to embody kingdom life, to be salt and light in the world to God's glory, and to stand like a wise person, built on solid rock.

Central to our discussion, the discourse first takes up the question of Jesus' relationship to the historic revelation of God in the Law and the Prophets (5:17-20). Jesus describes that relationship as "fulfillment." Jesus and his disciples in their teaching and behavior will not only not "abolish" that earlier revelation, but they will also "fulfill" it. And in the process (1) their righteousness will exceed that of the scribes and Pharisees, and (2) they will find themselves part of (will "enter") the kingdom of heaven (5:17-20). According to Matthew 5:21-48 this fulfillment will involve: (1) subordinating both Pharisaic tradition and the law of Moses to the word of Jesus ("You have heard...but I say"); (2) living not simply the Law but the Lawgiver's intent, the principle expressed in the Law; and (3) finally, with its importance underscored by its climactic position, it will involve seeking to embody the character of the Father himself in love transcending social-cultural barriers, a mode of kingdom life called "perfect" (5:43-48).

In these materials Matthew expressly addresses the question of evaluation. He gives direction to the sort of reflection Jesus' disciples must do on previous biblical revelation, and provides specific content for some critical aspects of that endeavor. Without continuing through the rest of the discourse, we see that in the process the loftiest expectations of kingdom life are put forward. This judgment of "loftiest expectations" is not imposed on the text or derived from our own positive response to this discourse. Rather it derives from the language and claims of the discourse itself. That is, in these attitudes and actions, Jesus' intended relationship to the historic Word of God is fulfilled. In these ways one "seeks first the kingdom of God" (6.34), "enters by the narrow gate" (7:13), and is finally "known" in judgment by the Son as Lord (7:21-23). Moreover, the climax of the entire book universalizes these instructions, placing them among the commands of Jesus to be observed by all the nations (28:18-20). Surely such material allows us to see basic issues of fundamental importance not only to Jesus but also to Matthew.

Turning to Romans 12–15, we see again how a book's structure and the explicit statements of the text enable one to discern foundational principles, profiles of God's highest will for his people against which other instruction and narrative in Scripture might be measured. The book of Romans itself divides into two major parts. In the first, Paul presents and defends the Good News as God's power to rescue creation alienated from God (1:18-11:39). In the second (12:1-15:13) he calls for reader response appropriate to the scope and grandeur of this Good News. (12:1-2 describes the core response.) This response will bring to a halt the readers' conformity to the fallen cultures of which they are a part ("the world"), and will issue in the ongoing "renewal" of their minds (12:2). He then treats particular arenas in which their conformity to the world will cease and in which their renewed mind will produce new approaches—in regard to themselves (12:3-8), to comrades in the faith and enemies (12:9-21), to governmental authority (13:1-7), to the centrality of love (13:8-10), to commitment (13:11-14), and to faith convictions (14:1-15:13).

These paragraphs present more than a set of miscellaneous admonitions appended loosely to Paul's theology. Rather this exposition of the love ethic is Paul's treatment of the renewed mind, the living sacrifice. This New Covenant ethic is summarized in the admonition to "owe no one anything, except to love one another" and in the claim that "love is the fulfilling of the law" (Rom. 13:8, 10, RSV), present implicitly or explicitly in all of the other paragraphs as well.

For our purposes we must now note carefully how Paul's statements and the book's structure emphasize the importance of this unit (12:1-15:13) as a resource for evaluation. For one thing, Paul calls the life described in this response a "living sacrifice, holy and acceptable to God," in essence a "worship life" (12:1). This will be life given to God, pleasing to him, and reflecting his character. These are lofty expectations indeed! Paul proceeds to claim that readers who respond with this "living sacrifice" will actually discern and do the will of God in various life experiences. They will embody life that is good, pleasing to God, and fulfilling of the purposes for which it was made and redeemed (12:2). This is an extraordinary claim!

Moreover, Paul offers this call (12:1-2, particularized in 12:3-15:13) explicitly ("therefore") on the basis of the Good News expounded in 1:18-11:36. Precisely *this* response and not another the apostle deems congruent with the Good News as he has presented it. Such response will not arise from a substantially different version of the Good News. And a substantially different response will not worthily appropriate this Good News. Indeed this "living sacrifice" response is itself an aspect of that Good News and part of God's saving grace to his creatures.

Our limited space prevents study of the other passages listed. Perhaps this will be sufficient to enable the student to see how the biblical writer's own statements and the structure of their works provide basis for evaluation.

Discern Biblical Preferences

Studying these and other passages it becomes clear that in the process of evaluation of biblical passages and of proposed interpretations one should:

- Take the personal over the mechanical.
- Take liberty over legalism.
- Take faith over works.
- Take holy love over all else.

These interlocking preferences surface continually, not only in the great outlines of God's highest designs for his people noted above, but throughout the entire Scripture, like threads in a tapestry. They are key insights that separate biblical revelation from its pagan environment and from distortions of biblical faith itself. As such they inform the evaluation process of determining which biblical ideas will take precedence over others.

Take the personal over the mechanical. This means choosing authentic, personal relationship between God and human beings and between persons themselves over against relationships governed or determined by strictly correct performance of certain acts. The foundational importance of this preference is implied already in the Genesis account of creation and "the deception" (Gen. 2:4-3:24). The creation account implies that human beings will have life and will know good and evil as they interact trustingly and obediently with the Creator and his word. It climaxes by celebrating open, authentic relationships between the first man and woman (2:4-24). The deception which alienated the first pair from God struck precisely at the point of the Creator's trustworthiness, and at the integrity of the woman and man's relationship with him (3:1-7).

God's major initiative to reestablish relationship with his creatures and ultimately to bless all the families of the earth began by inviting Abram to a relationship built primarily on trust and obedience, not on any specific "religious" activity or liturgical practice (Gen. 12:1-3). Specifically this became an invitation to "walk before" God with complete integrity (Gen. 17:2). This understanding of how the Creator and human beings should relate makes covenant faith possible and is one of its signal features. It absolutely rejects the essentially magical, mechanical notions of divine-human relationships dominant in ancient Near Eastern religions.

This charter stance of covenant faith surfaces repeatedly. (A few illustrations must do.) The Sinai covenant assumes this sort of authentic relationship. Several of its core commands safeguard this relationship, particularly the first, asking uncompromised allegiance, and the third, prohibiting frivolous use of God's name in oaths (Exod. 20:3, 7). The book of Deuteronomy understands covenant life in relational terms, chiefly as an expression of love and reverence for God and as a response to his own faithful love for Israel (Deut. 6:5; 7:6-11; 11:1 ff., etc.). In this book God anticipates that some might be tempted to think they could observe God's commands so as to "get the blessings," while actually harboring rebellion and deception in their hearts. He rejects outright such inauthentic "relationship" (Deut. 29:18-21). Yahweh cannot be coerced, manipulated, or deceived.

This reality undergirds the prophets' repeated rejection of perfunctory worship, a true oxymoron (e.g., Isa. 1:10-17; Amos 5:21-24; 8:4-6; Mic. 6:6-8). It surfaces in Jesus' call for authentic devotion that sets no stock in many words or religious appearance, but seeks to speak and live honestly with God (Matt. 6:1-18). Thus, from the very outset and in many different settings, Scripture reveals a preference for the personal and the authentic over the mechanical, the magical, and the perfunctory.

Take liberty over legalism. This means choose the freedom to bring love and grace creatively to bear at each step of life over the temptation to think salvation can be earned or godliness measured by strict adherence to God's law or Jesus' teaching. Scripture's emphasis on authentic, "personal" relationship with God did not imply that this relationship lacked moral content or abandoned moral transformation of human beings. As we have seen, Abraham's trust relationship with God involved obedience to God's word (Gen. 22:15-18). And the prophets who rejected perfunctory worship called not only for doing justice, but also for religious observance with integrity (cf. Malachi). Thus admonition abounds in Scripture regarding obedience to God, zeal in keeping Christ's commands (John 15:9-17; cf. 3:36), and fervor in holy living (2 Cor. 7:1).

Pitfalls arise, however. The temptation recurs to lose sight of the authentic trust relationship of which obedience is the expression. Human beings seem prone to forget the justice, mercy, and love which specific injunctions of Scripture intend to effect, and thereby fail to assimilate Scripture's own priorities (recall Amos 5:21-24; cf. Rom. 14:17-23). We are tempted to think that salvation consists in keeping the law (Gal. 3-4). We are inclined to develop religious traditions intended to safeguard the faith but actually at odds in the end with the fundamental principles of old and new covenant life (Mark 7:1-23). We wind up either sidestepping or actually contradicting the Lawgiver's intent (Mark 7:9-13). We take these matters seriously enough that we condemn others, even brothers and sisters in the faith, who do not concur with our conscience even in specific matters of custom or tradition (Rom. 14).

In the face of these temptations biblical writers repeatedly call the reader to remember the priorities of justice, mercy, and holy love implied by the character of God himself and by his acts on our behalf. They call readers to embody these qualities in their lives (Matt. 23:16-24; Rom. 14:13-23; Col. 2:16-23). They set before the church these general qualities as priorities and encourage disciplines of devotion and worship which will nurture them (Col. 3:12-17). They cite the attitudes and behavior of Jesus himself as the final yardstick by which believers may judge their particular conscience or culture (Rom. 14:15; 1 Cor. 8:11-12; Eph. 4:21; 5:2). These approaches support the preference of godly liberty over legalism.

Take faith over works. This means accent the establishment and nurture of unqualified, unwavering trust in God, and view upright behavior as an expression of that trust (Gen. 22:12; Gal. 5:6). Two realizations give perspective here. First, the very separation of "faith" from "works" presents something of a biblical oddity. Biblical writers rarely distinguish "faith" from "works" except specifically to treat the analytical question as to the *means* by which human beings are rescued. Are we saved by our own efforts to do God's will (keep the law, obey Messiah, etc.) or solely by trusting God? Romans 3:9-31 and Galatians 3:1-14 present such analyses. They emphasize trust as the sole means by which persons appropriate the saving grace of God.

Second, the word "trust" often translates better than "have faith/faith" or "believe/belief" the idea at stake in these words. Only rarely in the Bible does "having faith" or "believing" involve simple agreement with a proposition, i.e., "to believe some*thing*." This does not deny the necessity, indeed the critical import, of believing specific things. Paul says believers confess that "Jesus is Lord" and believe that "God has raised him from the dead" (Rom. 10:9-10). John claims persons who deny that "Jesus is the Messiah" or that "Jesus Messiah has come in the flesh" are liars and antichrist persons (1 John 2:22; 4:2). And the writer of Hebrews says that those who "would draw near to God must believe that he exists and that he rewards those who seek him" (Heb. 11:6, RSV). But almost always, and even in the book contexts from which these texts come, these faith affirmations are *assumed* as an integral part of a life fully entrusted to God, a faith *life*.

Paul's foundational claim in Romans 1:16 is but one of many cardinal expressions of this integration: "I am not ashamed of the gospel: it is the power of God for salvation to everyone who *lives in faith*," i.e., who *lives trusting God fully* for salvation (emphasis added; cf. 3:21-22). By citing Abraham as the parade example of this faith (Rom. 4), Paul expounds it as a journey in which all of life flows from profound trust in God (recall Gen. 12:1-9; 15; 22). It is to persons who would deny this faith life that James actually claims we are set right with God "by works and not by faith alone" (James 2:24, RSV; cf. 14-26).

From these perspectives biblical writers repeatedly emphasize this faith life itself with certain encourgements. Resist the inclination to compare oneself with others, particularly in order to establish orders of saintliness or adequacy in discipleship, they warn (Mark 9:33-37; 1 Cor. 4:1-5; Rom. 2). Resist overly self-conscious approaches to the sacrifice and obedience entailed in discipleship (Mark 10:28-31). Emphasize the grace of God and the power of his Spirit to effect character transformation in human beings (Eph. 2:1-9). And resist inclinations to boast about the miracles of character change that do occur in those who trust God, but boast rather in God himself (1 Cor. 1:26-31). In so doing one will accent the faith life over preoccupation with the works as ends in themselves.

Take holy love over all else. Repeatedly biblical writers, particularly but by no means exclusively New Testament writers, point readers to holy love as the goal of the entire salvation enterprise: love for God and for one another. As we have already seen, entire books of Scripture focus on this theme. Deuteronomy, we recall, presented Israel's whole response to God's own love as loving Yahweh their God with all their heart, all their soul and all their strength (Deut. 6:5). Jesus cited this command and God's instruction to "love your neighbor as yourself" (Lev. 19:18) as key to the entire law and prophets (Matt. 22:34-40). As noted earlier, the "fulfillment" of the law to be found in Jesus and his disciples reaches its apex in love patterned after God's character (Matt. 5:44-48). John, who attributes God's sending of the Son to his love, records the new covenant's "new command" as modeled after the Son's own love (John 3:16; 13:34), and elaborates these themes in the succeeding chapters (John 13-17). As we saw, implicitly and explicitly Paul expounds the "new mind" of those who respond to Good News as "living sacrifices" as essentially the life of holy love (Rom. 12:9 ff.; 13:8-10; cf. 15:1-7). While 1 Corinthians reaches its doctrinal climax in chapter 15, it reaches the climax of its response to the core problem plaguing the divided Corinthians in chapter 13, the "more excellent way" of holy love. Ephesians presents the believers' walk of love as the very purpose for God's saving deeds (Eph. 1:3-5, following the preferred punctuation of the KJV, ASV, NKJV, NAB, JB) and the object of Paul's prayer (Eph. 3:14-21). Book after book could be cited with major thematic or structural attention to claim that the purpose of God's saving work in the world is to bring about a loving response from his creatures, expressed in holy love for one another. I have used the expression "holy love" to highlight the covenantal character of this love—love filled with justice, faithfulness, purity and integrity, but love nonetheless.

Thus, if some proposed construal of Scripture urges an application of holiness that is not loving, neither is it an adequate understanding of biblical holiness. Appropriations of Scripture must be rejected if they render one's walk with God more mechanical than personal. If they make one more dependent on external conformity to isolated biblical phrases than on dynamic relationship with God, the applications envisioned are deficient. They simply do not reflect the deepest biblical concerns. In short, one may well have missed the point of the Bible!

Let Jesus Be the Judge

When asking whether the actions and attitudes modeled or commended in any specific part of the Scripture are to be applied to the life of the Christian, evaluate them by the standard of Jesus' life and words as understood in the New Testament. This principle is supported by two facts. First, Jesus clearly presented himself as Lord of all revelation. For example, he authoritatively revised the revelation through Moses, (Mark 7:19; 10:4 ff.; Matt. 5:21-48). Second, the apostles clearly wrote taking Jesus as the norm for life in the kingdom (e.g., Phil. 2). For Christians this proves to be the most critical stance for the evaluation task, hence this chapter's name.

Reading Psalm 139, one may model the psalmist's clear disowning of evil and decisive dedication to God (vs. 21-22). But one may not hate evil persons, or anyone for that matter, in spite of the various statements about hating persons scattered throughout the Bible (e.g., Ps. 5:5; Luke 14:26). The apparent difficulties posed in some of these references yield to sound interpretation. Others, like that in verse 22 of this psalm, do not. The "perfect" hatred in verse 22 (RSV, KJV) is "complete" hatred, not somehow "acceptable." That was perhaps adequate for the psalmist, but not for disciples of Jesus, as the Master and the apostles clearly state (cf. Matt. 5:21-26, 43-48 again and Rom. 12:9-21; 13:8-10). There is no fundamental "contradiction" between the psalmist's attitudes and those taught by Jesus. There is a chasm of several centuries in which the Father taught more perfectly his will, showing more adequate ways to express clear renunciation of evil and decisive dedication to God.

Recognizing such updates in revelation, seeing the differences, and selecting the higher way for application to the life of the Christian is precisely what is involved constantly in deciding how the life-giving Word will be lived out in our day. Let Jesus be the judge. That will not end all questions, nor should it be made a cliché substitute for careful observation and clear thinking. But it will go a long way toward helping one evaluate biblical passages consistently and toward guiding the process of understanding the diversity in biblical revelation.

Listen to the Canonical Dialogue

Sorting out the diversity in Scriptural revelation is much like listening to an inspired dialogue or a round table discussion within the canon of Scripture. One might visualize all the biblical writers—Moses, David, Amos, Isaiah and the other prophets, along with Matthew, Mark, Luke, John, Paul and others—seated around a large conference table, with Jesus, the risen Lord, at the head of the table, chairing the discussion. In evaluation one brings a passage one has interpreted to the discussion in order to listen to the overall dialogue in the canon on the issues raised by the passage. Depending on the passage in question and the issues involved, the discussions move differently, with different speakers addressing the question directly and indirectly. Around some there is thorough agreement. On some, the discussion moves essentially along a single direction, mainly achieving refinement and expansion of earlier points. On others there is considerable debate, with resolution only reached toward the end of the discussion.

On some issues the canonical dialogue appears not to have reached resolution. This does not mean that biblical revelation proves to be an inadequate guide for life (cf. 2 Tim. 3:16) or that God somehow "stopped speaking too soon." It has rather to do with the historical nature of the Bible and the apparent priorities of the One who inspired it. In the one case, because of its historical nature, the specific ethical and moral dilemmas of every age and culture cannot have been explicitly addressed. In the other case, God has focused full attention on his saving acts to reconcile an alienated world to himself, providing everything necessary to understand those acts and respond to them, and in his wisdom leaving other items less conclusively treated.

Slavery is an example of a topic on which the canonical dialogue seems, in the providence of God, not to have reached conclusion. Old Testament Torah and New Testament pastoral instruction providing for slavery, on the one

hand, seem to stand in tension with other teaching throughout the Bible (e.g., regarding creation and salvation) imply-
ing the rejection of slavery on the other hand. The question
spawned several centuries of debate in the church. God's
people finally concluded that even though the biblical conversation had not fully resolved the issue, careful, prayerful
"listening" could discern the *direction* of the discussion. The
canonical dialogue was heading toward the abolition of slavery. This target toward which the biblical conversation was
moving along a discernible trajectory finally became the conscience of the church—not because of Scripture's specific
teaching on slavery itself, but because of the implications of
other more fundamental instruction in the Bible and because
of the direction in which the whole canonical conversation
was seen to be moving.

Slavery not only provides a clear example of the need to
discern the biblical dialogue, but it is a particularly important
one. Its importance lies in the fact that it is now history. The
church's use of the Bible in the slavery controversies of the
eighteenth and nineteenth centuries is a well studied matter
of record, and thus provides experience from which we can
learn and take courage.

This case study in evaluation proves enlightening,
because in it one confronts the true diversity in Scripture on
the topic of slavery and related issues. This specific biblical
data informs ideas of inspiration and deepens concepts of the
Bible's essential unity. It encourages, because it shows that
inquiries on these matters can come to satisfactory conclusion.

After all our effort to understand the Bible adequately, it
would be possible to use the idea of a canonical dialogue to
undercut the whole process and sidestep biblical teaching.
Appeal to some conclusion beyond the canon could allow
readers to evade instruction unacceptable to them for whatever reason. This is certainly possible. But such an abortion
of Bible study is no more necessary here than in the process

of interpretation where it is equally possible. One *can* make the text say what one wants it to say, if one chooses to do so. Instead, students must be guided by the evidence here, just as in the process of determining the historic meaning of the text.

Find the Dialogue

Clearly the task of evaluation presents a formidable challenge to every student of Scripture. Beginning Bible students may find themselves particularly overwhelmed by the task. But experienced students also stretch to reach satisfactory results, for here even more than in interpretation, one seeks to bring the entire Scripture to bear upon one's understanding of the whole.

How do I know where to find the other biblical passages treating the same issues being dealt with in a passage I have interpreted? This question looms large before students with little knowledge of the Bible and remains a challenge to all. Since significantly related passages may not share much common vocabulary, the best resource in the long term is a life of study of the sort taught in this book. One will begin to know passages by their major concerns, by the main issues they address. Thus, one will know to bring together Genesis 1 and 2, Job 28, Proverbs 8, Isaiah 40, John 1, and Romans 1 around the topic of "creation" or "God the Creator," whether they share vocabulary or not.

Resources for Evaluation

• Concordances

• Cross-references

• Commentaries

• Bible dictionaries

• Dictionaries of theology

Using a concordance one can locate passages that share key words with the passage one is evaluating. Partners in Scripture study can help at this point. Cross-references in study Bibles will cite passages considered by the editors to relate significantly to one's passage. Major commentaries can also assist us here. Often the passages cited by commentators as resources for understanding a passage's meaning can also prove useful for evaluating it, for placing it in the flow of biblical revelation and for tuning into the biblical dialogue. Bible dictionaries and encyclopedias, and dictionaries of theology can also help gather passages related to the topic treated in a passage you are working on.

These more interpretive resources are useful at this point in two ways. First, they can help you know what passages you yourself should consider when attempting to place your passage in the canonical conversation. Second, these resources may well give you not only interpretive opinion but also evaluative insight. That is, they may tell you not only what they think a passage means but also how it participates in the canonical dialogue. The less experience one has in Scripture study, the more he or she will need to listen carefully to these resources for evaluation. They remain respected colleagues in study, even for students of long experience. In evaluation, as in interpretation, not only consultation but group *conversation* will often prove necessary to reach sound conclusions. The church's struggle over slavery represents one such extended conversation.

In this business of "letting Jesus be the judge," as in the other phases of Scripture study, one need not be paralyzed by what one does not know. Rather one can begin the process where one is, and add piece by piece to one's understanding of the Scripture's amazing, internal conversation and one's familiarity with the resources available to help in the listening.

This chapter, perhaps more than any other in *Bible Study That Works*, involves far-reaching assumptions in method and theology. But we have not thereby left the topic of Bible study and simply gone to theology. Our opening perspective (chapter 2) committed us to include application as an indispensable feature of Scripture study. Asking the "So what?" question makes some treatment of this "pre-application" reflection necessary.

So here, as at every other stage of process we are outlining, we invite the student to test what we say by their own study of the Bible. Test the evidence cited. Determine by your own careful study the nature of the Bible's unity and diversity. Come to your own conclusions regarding its own clues for managing this task of letting Jesus be the judge.

For further study read Traina, *Methodical Bible Study*, 201-213.

Chapter 6

Live the Word

Raise the "So What?" Question

Living the Word: This is the goal of the entire process. Good Bible study is much more than an academic pursuit. It aims at human transformation by the power of God's Word and Spirit. So having come to some conclusion as to the meaning of a passage (interpretation), and having gained some insight regarding the enduring significance of a biblical passage (evaluation), one must proceed to ask and answer the second question raised at the outset of our study: What does this have to do with us and with our world? (Chapter 2 on "What Are the Basic Questions?")

We deliberately raise this second basic question for several reasons. First, we do so because the process of discovering what a biblical passage means (interpretation) and applying it to our lives (application) are two different though dynamically related processes. We do well to separate them so as to give adequate attention to what the text actually does say and mean, without rushing prematurely to superficial or even erroneous applications. Secondly, we separate interpretation and application to help us understand the overall balance of adequate Scripture study. At some public and private Bible study we may devote more attention to understanding a passage, with minimal attention to present application. At other times more energy may be devoted to discerning applications for contemporary life. Neither is more important than the other. So extended inquiry into the text's meaning is not "irrelevant" or "bookish." Serious concern for present application of the Word does not mean "preoccupation with relevance." Both constitute part of a larger process of good Bible study.

Nevertheless, adequate Bible study must include the embodiment of that ancient Word in the contemporary reader. In fact, in some cases it may well be impossible to understand a text as it should or could be grasped until one has begun its application. This ancient conviction, reinforced in the latter half of the twentieth century, constitutes another reason we must deliberately raise the application question. Although we have legitimately laid out in sequence separate, broad "steps" or "phases" in Bible study, Scripture study is actually a dynamic process with complex interaction between the "steps." This fact bears particularly on application. We have rightly stressed the separation of interpretation from application. We have also concluded that significant understanding of written texts is possible without first hand experience of the text's content (else the use of Scripture in evangelism would be impossible). But the fact that common sense and the interpreter's own experience stood among the resources for finding answers to our questions about the text's *meaning* implies that, at least in some cases, application may actually contribute to fuller understanding of the text. Dimensions of some texts cannot be fully understood until they are "lived." Thus, while much application may occur rather intuitively, we do not leave it to chance. All Bible study at some stage should proceed to ask the enduring significance of the truth encountered and its relationship to the lives of the present readers.

Apply Major Principles First

Just as one is well advised to interpret main points first and consider details in the light of the whole, so it is in applying the Word. It is best to identify the central concerns of a passage and the general principles being enunciated and to ask regarding the significance of these matters for contemporary life. Then one may proceed to various details of the passage which may or may not apply to our day. In this way one will often perceive which features of a passage are of universal and transcultural significance, and which are more culture-specific and confined in application to a specific time and place in the past.

For example, in Matthew 6 the evangelist presents Jesus' approach to the question of authentic devotion to God— how one ought to "practice piety" (v. 1). In the process he presents the specific examples Jesus gave that were relevant to first century Jews: giving alms (vs. 2-4), prayer in the synagogues and on the street corners (vs. 5-6), non-Jewish verbosity in prayer (vs. 7-15), and fasting (vs. 16-18). The *principle* being taught in each appears to be that true worship and all practices related to it are to be done sincerely to God himself, without regard for impressing either people or God. Only this worship receives reward. Any other "worship" is in fact not worship, but an exercise done "to people" and rewarded by the fact that they observed it.

This principle would appear to apply to all cultures and all generations of believers. It does so in spite of the fact that many cultures and generations do not have synagogues, do not have the custom of public prayer on the street corners even by the pious, are not accustomed to highly repetitive and verbose prayer in pagan worship, are not familiar with religious fasting, and so on. Not only the general principle is applicable, but its application to the specific sorts of matters raised by Jesus is also valid: to practices of giving, however they are done and by whatever name they are called in different cultures, to public and private prayer, to pious practices such as fasting. Beyond this, the principle would be applicable to whatever cultures one might name.

Sometimes this practice of applying the major principle first is done almost intuitively in a sort of cultural transfer that "foreign" readers make in an attempt to transform what they are reading into understandable equivalents in their own culture. Beyond this intuitive process, the serious student will deliberately and consistently seek to discover the central principles being set forth and will apply them first, governing application of the details of the passage by direction set by the principle. Otherwise the application of the details may even, in some instances, contradict the force of the principle. So, for instance, even if a person understood the central principle in Matt. 6:1-18 of unpretentious worship, if he or she sought to carry that out by anointing their head (v. 17) with oil, in North American society the resulting hairdo would call more attention to itself than would a sad countenance. Some other cultural equivalent will have to be found to carry out the principle in this case!

Apply Ideas and Actions

Through Scripture God wills to shape both our ideas and our actions, not just one or the other. Both our inner and outer lives, our thoughts, beliefs, and "world views" as well as the actions which flow from those life convictions present agendas for spiritual growth and transformation. Moreover, the complex and important connection between our inner and outer lives underscores the import of attending carefully to scriptural instruction for both. Every reader of Scripture is a theologian, reading already with certain understandings of God, of the universe, of humankind and their relationship to God and one another. Derived from various sources, conscious and unconscious, adequate and inadequate, our "theologies" stand in need of correction, refinement, expansion. Beyond this, the frequent discord between our "espoused theology" (the ideas we *think we have* about God) and our "lived theology" (the ideas we *show we actually have* by our actions) hints at the considerable room for reflection we will find in applying Scripture in ideas and actions. Thus we attend carefully to the theology of worship and piety presented in Matthew 6 to shape both our ideas about such things and to guide our own actions.

Moving in application from ideas to actions often involves allowing principles discerned in Scripture to take form in the details of our lives. The principles themselves, clearly planted in our consciousness, provide bases for spontaneous applications all along the way. They become points of reference in our minds which are being renewed after the image of Christ. But these principles take on greater significance as we give consideration to specific and concrete ways in which they will be lived out for us.

Thus, if I am assured that God desires in my culture the same authentic worship described by Jesus in Matthew 6 and by many other biblical writers—unpretentious, without hypocrisy, and directed solely to the King who alone is worthy of worship—I will give attention to the specific ways that will influence my worship acts and attitudes. I will ask how my worship can be less hypocritical, less pretentious, less for those around me, and more for the King.

So it must be for all truth of Scripture. The student should think in terms of specific, concrete, dollars and cents, time and energy investments, of specific relationships with persons and organizations and possessions, of the real stuff out of which his or her life is made, as the arena where the Word will take shape today. Significant applications will not occur in vague realms of "spirituality" or "holiness" that have nothing to do with life as it is lived.

Apply Corporately and Individually

Western and particularly North American culture's individualism leads many to think first of God's Word to them individually. The encouragement of independent, direct study of Scripture by individuals of this work reflects this culture in part. While God certainly cares about the response of individuals to his Word, most of Scripture itself aims at the transformation of *communities* and individuals as members of those communities. We need not impose an artificial barrier between community and individual, as though urging individuals to appropriate biblical teaching somehow sabotaged Christian community. Rather we aim to enhance each individual's awareness of his or her dynamic relationship with the several communities and to heighten believing communities' awareness of their responsibility to the persons who make them up.

In Scripture repeatedly these appear in marvelous balance, such as when Moses addressed the thousands of Israelites on the plains of Moab. Moses calls the nation to covenant, directing the Lord's central command at both the nation and its individuals: "Hear, O Israel [addressing the nation]: The LORD our God, the LORD is one. Love the LORD your God with all your heart and with all your soul and with all your strength" [The pronouns and verbal referent are all singular!] (Deut. 6:4-5, NIV). So adequate application thinks both of how the Bible shapes *my* ideas and actions and also of how it must shape the ideas and actions of the several *communities* of which I am a part—home, town, clubs, schools, businesses, associations, state and federal government, and the social, political, and legal structures that shape them.

Apply Positively and Negatively

Scripture applies both positively and negatively to our lives. God, through his Spirit and the Word, both affirms and rebukes, comforts and confronts, assures and unsettles, much as he did through the prophet Jeremiah (Jer. 1:10). Because of the power of God's grace at work in his world, we should be surprised if we never sense affirmation through his Word: "Your confidence in my providence, like Joseph's [Gen. 50:15-21], is sound, my son," or "Your trust in me, like Mary's [Luke 1:26-38], pleases me, my daughter." On the other hand, because of the realities of the human condition, we should be suspicious if we never find ourselves unmasked, our sin exposed before the living God in his Word: "My child, like John [Mark 9:38-41], you seem so quick to exclude from my blessing those who are not following your group," or "Dear one, in this matter of _____, you seem to think so much like the world from which you have been rescued" [Eph. 4:17-24]. So across the broad range of ideas and actions to which your study of Scripture will relate, expect the Word to impact your life both positively and negatively.

Get started with Probes and Questions

Scripture truth intersects our lives in ways as varied as the myriad combinations of those truths and our complex lives. As we have seen, at times the Word of God convicts us of sin. At other times God speaks assurance through his Word. Sometimes our ways are condemned, sometimes confirmed. At other points we are instructed, given new information and understanding of both the past and present, and so on. If one is at a loss to know just how to start bringing the truth of a passage to the present, two suggestions may at least help one get underway: 1) exploring a "whole-life application probe," and 2) asking application questions. They are only suggestive, but can provide a starting place.

1. *Whole-life application probe.* Visualize a figure with a circle in the middle and lines running out from it like spokes in a wheel to all the different aspects of human existence in this universe—sociology, psychology, theology, economics, science, law, government, politics, ecology, arts, entertainment, media, for example. Or you might prefer less abstract labels for these sectors of life and thought. Then think of placing the instruction from the passage you have studied and evaluated in the center circle, with the lines leading you to ask what that teaching might have to do with each major facet of human life before God.

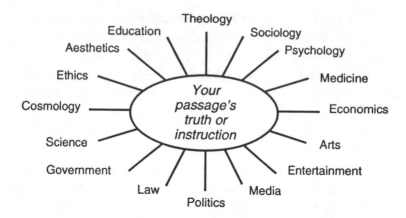

"Walk around" the circle, probing whether and how the particular teaching might impact your understandings of concepts of God, his being, character, and relationship to the universe and its creatures (theology); how human beings relate to one another (sociology); personality development and dysfunction (psychology); problems of health and medical treatment and services (medicine); the use and management of money—your money, your county's or country's or the world's (economics); and so on around the circle.

Of course few single biblical instructions will impact all of these areas of life; most will relate clearly and directly to a few, and less directly to some more, only remotely if at all to others. The point here is not to force relevance but rather to expand one's horizons with regard to the possible impact of Scripture upon the contemporary world.

2. *Application questions.* Having concluded study of a passage, one might begin the application process by asking:

a. What affirmations should I make in light of this word—about God, about Jesus of Nazareth, about myself and others, about this world?

b. In what ways does this passage confirm good already present by God's grace in my life?

c. What sin should I confess in view of this passage?

d. What changes should I make in my investment of time, money, energy, or personal resources in view of the truth of this passage?

e. What prayer should I pray for myself, my family, my friends, and my enemies in light of what I have seen in the Word?

Continue the process in prayer and meditation before the Master whose Word you have studied. There is literally no end to what Jesus called "hearing and doing" his Word (Matt. 7:24).

Review the Process

With this guidance in applying God's Word we conclude the core of *Bible Study That Works*, the outline of studying Scripture presented in Part Two. Instead of starting with this application goal of the project, we set out in Chapter 3 by encouraging Bible students to begin by observing carefully the content and structure of Scripture units and to distinguish between seeing what is actually there and discerning what the text means. We gave particular attention to the various relationships which structure biblical units and their role in guiding our study.

Based on this "seeing" of the text, in Chapter 4 we examined the questions which form the bridge between seeing what the text says and discovering its meaning, i.e., between observation and interpretation. We then explored the sources of evidence for answering those questions, sources beyond ourselves (context, the form and use of terms, author's intent, historical setting, other interpreters) and sources within ourselves (spiritual discernment, common sense, experience).

Then, in Chapter 5, before moving to the living of the Word, we considered the problem of sorting out the diversity found within the Bible's essential unity, the problem of *which* word to live out on a given topic. This involved understanding the flow of biblical revelation, separating the local from that of universal significance, discerning biblical preferences, and finding and listening to the canonical dialogue so as to "let Jesus be the judge."

Finally, in Chapter 6 we returned to the "So what?" question and discussed the business of living the Word, beginning with major principles. We suggested applying the Word of God in ideas and actions, corporately and individually, positively and negatively, with probes and questions to start the endeavor.

This basic program of Scripture study raises many questions, and opens the door to much more inquiry. To these matters of follow-up we now turn.

For further study read Traina, *Methodical Bible Study*, 214-219.

Chapter 7

Study Informed by the Bible's Own Story

Use of contemporary versions is commonplace for many, but for others the matter still presents a puzzle and provokes consternation. Where there is debate, it usually proceeds along lines of arguing the relative "accuracy" of particular versions. The adequacy and usefulness of specific versions can indeed be argued. But the verdicts rendered seldom relate simply to "accuracy" or "faithfulness to the original." The translators'/revisers' goals and their chosen approach to translation (on the spectrum from formal to dynamic equivalence) figure substantially in the discussion.

The reasons offered in chapter 2 for studying Scripture in your own dialect are matters seldom given sufficient weight in ordinary, lay discussions of text selection. These are essentially theological and historical reasons, not primarily translation theory reasons. They have to do largely with taking seriously the story of the composition and transmission of Scripture to us. The Bible's own story provides a model that puts the discussion of versions in an entirely different frame. The following discussion expands on the outline in chapter 2 by presenting further thoughts on the "Does God use 'thees' and 'thous'?" question.

Take the Pattern of Biblical Revelation Seriously

First, study in your own dialect *to take the pattern of biblical revelation itself seriously.* This pattern reveals *God's commitment to communicate.* God spoke to people in varying cultures and in succeeding centuries in the language of their own day, not in previously canonized, "sacred languages." Linguistic developments within the Bible itself readily attest to this fact. The period from Abraham and Moses to the close of the Old Testament spanned more than a millennium, with another four to five hundred years to the close of the New Testament. Still, those portions of the biblical text which have retained their earliest linguistic form, for example Exodus 15 and Judges 5, stand in obvious contrast to their literary settings. It is clear that having begun the written revelation in archaic Hebrew, or more likely in Amorite or some earlier language, God did not hesitate to inspire succeeding biblical authors to change the language forms in order to communicate in the dialects of their day.

Thus, the historical narratives of Samuel and Kings incorporate materials from much older sources such as the royal archives which went all the way back to the time of David (see, e.g., 1 Kings 11:41 and 14:29). But the historians of Samuel and Kings revised the older sources to read in the Hebrew of the time of the exile when these histories of Israel were put into their final form, a revision comparable to putting Wycliffe's translation of the Bible (fourteenth century English) into modern idiom.

The inspired change from Hebrew to Aramaic and then to Greek in the Bible is similar. The earlier Old Testament books were penned in Hebrew. But as Aramaic became the common language of diplomacy and commerce and finally of daily speech in the Eastern Mediterranean and Mesopotamian lands (in the period of the exile), biblical books began to appear in Hebrew heavily influenced by Aramaic, with portions actually in Aramaic, the official language of the Persian empire. The books of Daniel, Ezra, Nehemiah, Esther, and Chronicles especially reflect this adaptation of God to the changing language of his people.

Finally, by the New Testament era, Greek had become the most widely used tongue of the biblical world. Given God's demonstrated commitment to communicate his Word in written form intelligible to the generation at hand, the result was predictable. No matter that God had inspired "holy men of old" to write in Hebrew and Aramaic—the Word of his Son would appear in Greek. And not only in Greek, but in *koine*—the "common" Greek of the marketplace, of legal documents, of personal and business correspondence, and even of the world's graffiti. Why? So people could read God's Word in the language of their own day and understand it as readily as any other contemporary documents.

Regarding the question "Does God use 'thees' and 'thous'?" the answer is perhaps a surprising but resounding "No!" As a matter of fact, Hebrew, Aramaic, and Greek have no special, "polite" forms of the personal pronouns with which one might address deity or respected persons (unlike German, for instance).

Nor does one find the biblical text preserving *archaic* forms of the personal pronoun in addressing God, although the option was certainly available to the biblical writers. This absence of archaizing pronouns throughout the Scripture, in narrative and discourse about God, as well as in prayer and praise to God is striking. The use of English "thy," "thee," and "thou," and related forms in prayer and in some modern Bible translation, is, of course, such an archaizing form of respect. In short, God inspired persons to address him in the same forms they used to talk to other intimate, contemporary friends, not in any special speech.

Why should you study the Bible in your own dialect? It takes seriously the inspired pattern of biblical revelation. God's own commitment to communication followed this pattern.

Keep Faith with the Translation Passion of the Church

Secondly, you should include a modern English version at or near the center of your Bible study *to keep faith with the translation passion of the Church*. This passion reveals *the saints' commitment to communicate.* Too many heated discussions defending one or another of the historic English versions as the most desirable English Bible for study and depreciating the use of other more recent English versions are divorced from a consideration of the church's work of preserving and transmitting the written Word of God. (Incidentally, the proper use of the historic versions in study needs no defense!) The passion of God's people to put his Word into the language and dialect of the contemporary readers has from the start led to an almost unending list of revisions and translations. This "translation urge" of the church was born of the very Spirit of God, as we have seen in the paragraphs above.

The appearance of this compulsion to update the biblical text did not even await the close of the older testament. Thus, while one may point to selected passages which for one reason or another have retained their earlier linguistic form, this is not generally the case. Spellings were systematically revised; verb and pronominal forms, updated. The process of textual revision was already underway before the biblical revelation was finished.

The same may be said for the translation of God's Word. Before the New Testament was even written, all or part of the Old Testament had already been translated into Greek (the Septuagint) and Aramaic (the Targum). Indeed, the Septuagint had itself undergone multiple revisions prior to the first Christian century. As if this were not enough, the history of the New Testament's textual transmission is even more awesome. One discovers that before a single syllable of the Bible had appeared in early "English" (late seventh century A.D. for sections in Anglo-Saxon), the New Testament had already been translated in whole or in part into Syriac, Latin, Coptic, Ethiopic, Armenian, Gothic, Georgian, Nubian, and no doubt other tongues as well.

When one turns from such facts to the claims of any one English version to monopolize the believer's attention, one almost feels a sense of shame at the arrogance, if not igno-rance, involved. The designation of any biblical version or revision as the church's best and last attempt to place the Word of God in the language of the people is a travesty on the labors and sacrifice of saints of bygone eras who gave even their lives in the desire to communicate. Why should you study the Bible in your own dialect? To keep faith with the passion of the church to communicate.

Appropriate the Power of God's Word in your Own Life

Finally, you should study the Scripture in your own tongue *to appropriate the power of God's Word in your own life.* Scripture should be *God's communication with you!* If you are to read God's Word with the immediate, contemporary, attention-demanding impact intended by the One who inspired it and supported by the church which transmitted it, you should study the Bible in your *own* language—not in the dialect of your ancestors. In your devotional and study habits as elsewhere in your religious exercises, you must resist like the plague any language or artificial roles that divorce faith and worship from daily life, from the home and market-place, and relegate them to "sacred" places, special times, and privileged lingo.

This refusal to compartmentalize human life, designating some parts sacred and open to God and others secular and out of the domain of God's interest and will constitutes one of Scriptures most consistent and important themes. Desig-nation of particularly sacred times and places in Scripture (e.g., Lev. 23-25) never implied artificial boundaries between these times and places and the entire life of the community, boundaries excluding God from "normal" life. On the con-trary, from earliest models God's will was that his people walk before him with integrity (or without blame) (Gen. 17:1), envisioning all of life open to God and lived for him.

So the reluctance to use language whose very form implies allocating "religion" to some out-of-the-ordinary sphere of life, removed from the central questions and concerns of daily existence rests on ancient revelation and conviction. God does not use "thees" and "thous." Why should you?

For interesting reading on these questions, consult John Beekman and John Callow, *Translating The Word of God* (Grand Rapids: Zondervan, 1974); Kathleen Callow, *Discourse Considerations in Translating The Word of God* (Grand Rapids: Zondervan, 1974); F. F. Bruce, *History of The Bible In English*, 3rd ed. (New York: Oxford University Press, 1978); and the series of articles under "Versions" in *The Anchor Bible Dictionary*, Vol. 6 (New York: Doubleday, 1992), 786-851.

Chapter 8

Integrate, Reach Out and Keep Digging

Readers of *Bible Study That Works* often raise questions which show their desire to integrate these studies into their present lives, to use the skills they have learned to help others, and to continue growing in their ability to interpret and live the Word. Here are the most common questions put to me from readers.

1. How does Bible study of the sort presented here relate to my devotional life and my devotional use of the Bible?

Two or three assumptions govern a response to this question. I assume, first of all, a long-term view of one's spiritual disciplines, long enough to make room for ebb and flow of life, long enough for patience and variety. This means that Scripture *study*, not simply Scripture *reading* can often form some part of my devotional life. Sometimes it stands at the heart of it; sometimes it is supplementary to other focuses. Classic Christian devotional experience counsels breadth and variety in the disciplines through which we invite God to shape our lives.[11] I assume an informal, written record, a journal or jottings from one's spiritual journey. This means one can take notes, sometimes very brief, at times more extensive, but always *cumulative*, building on previous insight, adding to previous discoveries. One could study a biblical book over several weeks or even months and not lose continuity or relevance. I assume almost infinite variety among fellow pilgrims, so that none of us should be bur-

---

[11]As seen so well in Richard Foster's *Celebration of Discipline: The Path to Spiritual Growth* (San Francisco: Harper & Row, 1978).

dened with precisely replicating another's work or way in such things as the use of Scripture in our devotional life.

Beyond these assumptions, *Bible Study That Works* is as much about a way of reading the Bible as it is about a method of study. It presents a stance toward Scripture that influences its use at every level, from rapid reading to painstaking analysis. So one does not have to be self-consciously "studying" the Bible to be enriched by the approach offered here. All of these considerations lead one to think the sort of study presented in *Bible Study That Works* can inform one's devotional life.

Perhaps the most important conviction undergirding this encouragement is the judgment that what God says to me personally and devotionally through the Bible as Scripture should agree with understandings of those texts fit for doctrine and instruction in the church and world as well. Of course, it is possible and quite common to use the Bible as simply one more "devotional classic" or "devotional book." In this case its passages could perhaps mean whatever I want them to mean, or whatever seems to "leap out at me," or whatever God may speak to me through prayer and meditation upon those texts. But the Bible has not historically been accepted by the people of God as simply one more among many devotional writings. Instead it has been seen as the revelation of the Living God, more than a mirror of the reader and more than a simple point of departure for meditation.

Thus, it is more a matter of disposition toward the text than methods of study which in the end determines the spiritual impact of Scripture. Openness, receptivity, patience, surrender, detachment, and willingness to move beyond analysis, problem solving, and the mastery of the text are needed.[12] In this receptivity the implications of the text will

---

[12]See M. Robert Mulholland, Jr., *Shaped By the Word* (Nashville: The Upper Room, 1985).

often be intensely personal and uniquely suited to one's situation, but consistent with an understanding of the text appropriate for the instruction of the church as a whole also.

2. How can I use this sort of Bible study in group study?

This depends on the nature of the group and the level of accountability of its members. Leading groups where few of the participants may be expected to come having studied the Scripture passage, one can still strengthen the church by modeling good use of Scripture in several ways. First, one can actually make the content and flow (design) of the passage itself, the issues raised by the passage, and their possible significance for today the basis for class discussion. Students are thus helped to see the relevence of Scripture to their own lives. Second, one can proceed as though it is possible to choose between alternative interpretations, and to do so based on evidence gleaned from the text and beyond. Such instruction counters the common idea that one interpretation of a passage is just as good as any other one, or that interpretation is a strictly private matter not open to group accountability. And third, one can be aware of the differences between seeing what is there, saying what it means, letting Jesus be the judge, and applying the Word to today. Persons are thus influenced to develop a similar flow in their own approach to the Bible. All of this is possible without explicitly talking to the class about method or concerning them with formal categories such as "observation" or "interpretation." My own experience with general lay groups (e.g., Sunday school classes, midweek "Bible study and prayer" meetings) has been that if I can help them just read a passage structurally, actually seeing what is there, where it starts, where it ends and how it gets there, amazing insight emerges, without one formal note of "method" or "structure."

In groups including some persons with higher accountability, one might even make certain stages of the interpretive process self-conscious group projects. In this case persons deliberately take on such projects as studying words, making a chart of content and/or structure, listening to the canonical dialogue to discern cross-cultural significance, or reflecting on various avenues of application. In any case one must take care that "method" itself (as opposed to Scripture) does not become the agenda, unless that is what the group wants to take on.

Bible Study That Works itself would prove most useful to persons interested not simply in Bible *study* but in *how* to study the Bible. Groups have had most success using the text in one of two ways: (1) as a resource for directly studying Bible study method; and (2) as a resource to enrich Bible study by adding a method component to the group agenda. Most success comes, I think, when persons actually studying the Bible are at the same time giving attention to *how* they are studying. So one might study chapter 3 on seeing what is there and dealing with units as a whole, and then put those insights to work in selected texts. Then read about seeing relationships, and return to the texts to find their design, and so on. This back and forth approach is modeled in the abbreviated study guide in chapter 9.

3. Where do I go beyond Bible Study That Works*? When I am prepared to move beyond the nontechnical approach to Scripture study presented here, what do I do and where do I look for help?*

Students can move beyond *Bible Study That Works* along several interrelated paths, all of which promise interesting and rewarding study:

(1) One can pursue legitimate, theoretical and theological questions attending almost every step of the process we have outlined. Some of these questions we have acknowledged but not pursued. Others have gone unmentioned in *Bible Study That Works*. These will for the most part be questions treated in more extensive works on hermeneutics, the study

of the entire endeavor of interpreting and understanding documents (and other modes of human communication), and, in Christian circles, the theological implications involved.

(2) One can pursue more extensively the explanations and instructions only briefly stated in this work. For example, in chapter 3 under "See What is There" we suggested observing the literary type and genre, barely scratching the surface of the sorts of literature found in Scripture, the various literary genres encountered and the impact of these matters on interpretation and even application. Or in that same chapter under "Look for the Design," these "relationships" and others can all be discussed more precisely, and the various types of structural relationships considered. Moreover, other sorts of "design," such as rhetoric and plot and character development present worthy matters for study.

(3) Certain advances in biblical study are open only to persons with competence in the biblical languages. Precise grammatical analysis, extensive word study, rhetorical analysis, close comparison of parallel and related passages, and many other features of Scripture study can be done with certainty only in the original language of the documents. This is no depreciation of careful study in the vernacular. But it does recognize the fact that some questions cannot be settled without using the original text. Learning these languages is within the grasp of most persons who are able to appreciate the types of questions which can only be answered with them.

Grant Osborne's book, *The Hermeneutical Spiral: A Comprehensive Introduction to Biblical Interpretation* (Downers Grove, IL: InterVarsity Press, 1991) offers an excellent treatment of these paths and many others. Extensive bibliography is found at every point, enabling one to pursue matters as far as one would like.

Chapter 9

Get Started with a Study Guide

The following study guide leads a student in applying to Psalm 139 the sort of Scripture study envisioned in *Bible Study That Works*. The study will be selective, leaving much work to be done. But it can give persons who are wondering where to begin at least a place to start. It illustrates the approach one can take to the whole psalm and to the rest of the Bible. The study is not totally open-ended, for at many points I have anticipated the observational or interpretive results to which I think the student will most likely come. At other points I have assumed a certain stance and steered the student in that direction. These anticipated results or directives often appear in the form of questions which already assume an interpretive or observational decision. Even so, it will illustrate much of what we have been writing about. At points where students conclude that the evidence better supports another decision, they should follow the evidence rather than the study guide. The task units proposed here can be divided into smaller units or collected for longer studies, as fits the student's schedule. The study guide assumes the student has access only to a Bible. Where we consult other resources, the study guide will provide needed information.

Getting Started

1. Open and close each time of study with prayer. At the outset offer your study to God as an expression of faith

106

and devotion, asking for the Spirit's assistance in gaining insight and in developing a truly teachable heart. Conclude each study with a prayer of thanks, appropriating whatever insights you have gained. These encouragements to prayer will be assumed for each of the following studies.

2. *Make careful observations and take notes.* Don't simply quote or repeat the text in your notes. *Describe* what you see. *Label* it. *Rephrase* it. This sounds elementary, but it is hard to exaggerate its importance for engaging your mind in the process.

3. Note the superscription (v. 1a), informing us that this prayer is also a song attributed to David. Thus, we have here a poem, not a simple narrative or discourse. Most modern versions present the text in a form reflecting this poetic genre. Hebrew poets placed thought lines in parallel relationship to one another, as in "You know when I sit down" followed by "And [you know] when I rise up" (verse 2, NRSV). This "parallelism" leads to a certain amount of apparent repetition (though careful study shows much significant difference between parallel lines). So you may expect an idea to be rephrased in several different ways. Reading for an overview, then, take care not to allow the rephrasings to sidetrack you. Wait for substantial turns in the road before concluding that a new topic is at hand.

4. In each study unit below, I suggest reading the whole unit before following the guides. Sometimes the items are best considered together and even carried out together, even though they must be listed separately.

Seeing the Content of Psalm 139

1. You may want to review "What Are the Basic Questions?" and "Study in Units" (ch. 2), along with "See What is There" (ch. 3).

2. Read Psalm 139 as a whole, with paper and pencil at hand. Jot down your initial, overall impressions and questions, without getting mired in details. What does the psalm as a whole seem to be about?

3. Identify the paragraphs and note two or three major matters of content in each one. To identify paragraphs, regard a series of verses that seem to be about the same or closely-related matters as paragraph units. To get started, you may want to follow the paragraph divisions in the version you are using. This study divides the psalm into four paragraphs, verses 1-6, 7-12, 13-18, and 19-24. Upon later study you may well revise your beginning divisions.

Some things may puzzle you in the psalm. Some ideas may seem difficult to accept or understand. At this point simply note such matters, and keep your attention on the general picture.

Incidentally, if you described paragraph 1 as talking about the Lord's "omniscience" go back and check again. The paragraph is not about the Lord's knowledge of everything in general, but about his amazing knowledge of the psalmist. Nor does the paragraph deny the Lord's knowledge of everything. It may even imply his omniscience. However, at this point we are looking for accuracy in observing what was actually written.

4. Give a short title to each of the paragraphs, and then to the psalm as a whole. Put the essence of the content of each unit into brief, memorable, accurate titles.

5. Experiment with presenting your findings to this point on a rough chart. It might look like this, arranged horizontally, across a full sheet of paper.

One could even use a "chart format" from the start. At the outset one would note the paragraphs and lay out the chart. Then record the main items from each paragraph in their place, followed by titling each paragraph and finally the psalm as a whole. In any case, at

Psalm Title _____

Paragraph titles			
Main ideas, items of content for each paragraph			

this point treat these as aids to study, roughly drawn for your own use, not works of art for public display.

6. What atmosphere does this poem carry? What emotions does the psalmist seem to express in this piece? Do you sense fear? Praise? Wonder? Anger? Anxiety? Where? Is there a movement or progression or change in the tone of the prayer? Where? From what to what?

7. What sort of prayer does this seem to be (the genre issue)? Is it basically a hymn of praise to the Creator? Is it a complaint in which the psalmist seeks to defend himself against enemies and to enlist God's help against them?

8. Make whatever other observations you wish to at this time. Who is speaking? To whom? Why does it appear that the psalmist speaks as he does?

9. Based on your present understanding of the psalm (which will grow and change with further study), what significance do you tentatively see in the main ideas voiced in this song?

Note: If we were studying a book of any size rather than a chapter-length unit, on this overview we would read noting a few main ideas of each chapter and giving titles to the chapters, rather than the paragraphs.

Starting to See the Design of Psalm 139

1. You may find it helpful to review the paragraphs on "Look for the Design: The Relationships" (ch. 3).

2. With one eye on your content notes, think your way through Psalm 139 again with an eye toward seeing how it goes together. This time, ask how each paragraph relates to the preceding one, or how the psalmist moves from one paragraph to the next. Discover what relationships tie the paragraphs together. In the process you will no doubt see the content with new clarity and will correct or add to your previous notes.

3. A good place to start in seeing relationships is to look for repeated words and ideas, since most units are tied together in part by repetition. What repetitions or themes tie this song together?

4. Note in the first paragraph, after the superscription, that the psalmist makes a general affirmation about the Lord's knowing him (v. 1). Then verses 2-5 give specifics, detailing various ways in which the Lord knows the psalmist. Finally, verse 6 gives the psalmist's response to these realizations, the result—a praise result—of those claims.

5. Does the second paragraph (verses 7-12) continue the theme of the Lord's knowing? If so, how? Do we find here more specifics of the Lord's knowing? How presented? (You may find it helpful to consider how the ideas in each paragraph go together in preparation for asking how the paragraphs themselves interrelate. In item 4 we began with this sort of consideration of the structure of the first paragraph itself, before moving to ask how the second related to it. Eventually you will want to see this more detailed movement, though at this point it may not help you. Proceed in the way that seems to help you most.)

6. Moving to paragraph 3 (verses 13-18), note the first word, "for." Judging by this word, how does the following

material about God's creation of the psalmist and the Creator's thoughts about the psalmist relate to the two opening paragraphs about his astounding knowledge of the psalmist?

7. Finally, consider how the closing paragraph (verses 19-24) flows out of the first three. Does it explain the previous material? Or does it build on the preceding paragraphs, offering a resulting set of petitions?

8. Add notes to your chart so it shows the design as well as the content of Psalm 139. That is, see if you can show not only the content but the progression of the thought in the psalm on your chart. Sometimes arrows, connecting lines, even colors are useful to make these connections.

9. If you have read many other songs, you recognized that the opening three paragraphs of the song (verses 1-18) sounded much like hymns you have encountered elsewhere, like Psalm 104. The closing verses (19-24), resembled prayers in which the psalmist protests innocence and cries out for deliverance from accusers, like Psalm 26 (even though no explicit prayer for deliverance shows up here). What possible significance do you see to this movement?

10. What insights have you gained into the meaning of the psalm as a result of seeing how it goes together? What significance do you see in these for your world? Do you see possible significance for persons who are falsely accused, for persons who are misunderstood by others, who may wonder if anyone understands them?

Asking Questions and Finding Answers (From the Text of Psalm 139 Itself)

1. You may find it helpful to review chapter 4 on "Asking Questions and Finding Answers."

2. Trying to focus questions on major matters of content and structure, we could ask the following questions:

a. What is involved in the Lord's knowledge of the psalmist? What does he know about the psalmist? What is assumed by these claims about the Lord's knowing—about the Lord? About the psalmist?

b. What possible limits or barriers to the Lord's knowing are considered in verses 7-12? How are they presented and what appears to be the point of raising them?

c. What is involved in God's creative activity according to this prayer (verses 13-18)? What do we know about the Creator from this poem? How does the psalmist relate that activity to his affirmations about the Lord's knowing of him? Why meditate about the Creator's making of the psalmist in the middle of this prayer? What do these findings imply?

d. What is involved in the psalmist's rejection of any sympathy for the Lord's enemies (verses 19-22)? Why might the psalmist voice his disdain so strongly? What does this imply about his relationship to the Lord?

e. What seems to be involved in the petition for God to "search...and know" the psalmist's heart (verse 23), in view of the emphasis earlier that the Lord does, as a matter of fact, "search...and know" him?

f. Does the first part of verse 24 imply, perhaps, that the psalmist is being accused or at least feels accused of some wrong? If so, what do these closing petitions in verse 24 imply? What would they suggest about the overall significance of the prayer?

3. So as not to be overwhelmed, just start "at the top," and work through as many questions as you can. Start this first round of answers by returning to the text of Psalm 139 itself. If we gather more information, draw conclusions based on what we find, and reflect further on those findings, we will go a long way toward answering our questions.

4. When you have done some of this work, note the main points of significance you are beginning to see for your own life and world.

Finding Answers from Information Outside Psalm 139

1. If we want to go beyond the understandings derived solely from our work with the psalm text, we will need to get more information. This information will most likely come from studying the use of key words or consulting resources that can give us background information. To illustrate, we'll start with items that appear puzzling.

2. What is the meaning of the strange word, "Sheol," in verse 7, and of the clauses, "If I take the wings of the morning" and "If I settle at the farthest limits of the sea," in verses 8-9? Verse 7 asks questions about places in which the psalmist might go beyond the Lord's presence, and presumably therefore outside of his "knowing presence" (in light of the concern of verses 1-6). Verse 8 raises possible answers and then denies they are options by affirming that God is even there: "If I ascend to heaven, you are there; if I make my bed in Sheol, you are there" (NRSV).

3. We will begin with our own study of the term, and consult other interpreters later.

   a. Consulting other versions, we find this word translated "Sheol" (RSV, JB, NEB), "the depths" (NIV), "hell" (KJV, NKJV), and "the nether world" (NAB). These raise our interest, but do not necessarily bring clarity.

   b. If we look our word up in Strong's *Concordance*, we will look up "hell," because Strong's works with the KJV. The key number of this word in Strong's *Concordance* turns out to be #7585. In the "Hebrew and Chaldee Dictionary" Strong provides in the back of his work, we discover the Hebrew word involved is actually *Sheol* and that this word is translated "grave, hell," and "pit" in the KJV. If we look up each of these words in turn (grave, hell, pit) and find all the #7585 references, we will have all the Old Testament occurrences of our word for study.

The Hebrew word *Sheol* occurs 65 times in the Old Testament. Perhaps we would limit our study to the fifteen occurrences in the Psalms (6:5; 9:17; 16:10; 18:6; 30:3; 31:17; 49:14,15; 55:15; 86:13; 88:3; 89:48; 116:3; 139:8; 141:7). This will give us at least a good sample of the word's use. We will look up each of these references in turn and examine the context of each occurrence, with this question in mind: "If all I knew about this word were what I could learn from this occurrence, what would I think it meant?" These samples can get you started.

In Psalm 6:5, *Sheol* appears to name a place where the dead in some way are, a place from which God should or could expect no praise, apparently because those there cannot render praise. *Sheol* here names a place from which the psalmist prays to be delivered. Saving his life, God would, in effect save him from *Sheol*.

In Psalm 9:17 *Sheol* names the place to which "the wicked" and whole "nations that forget God" depart at their death. This fate, it appears (v. 16) is part of the judgment of God.

In 16:10 *Sheol* is parallel to "the pit" (RSV) and names the place to which the Lord does not "give up" the psalmist. Here "not giving someone up to sheol" means the Lord preserves his life and protects him (verses 5-9).

In 30:3 *Sheol* again stands parallel to "the pit," and names a place to which persons go at death. The psalmist praises the Lord because he has "brought up my soul from Sheol" (RSV). In light of verse 2, this apparently means the Lord has healed him—not that

God resurrected him from actual death. This godly man, then anticipated going to Sheol, had the Lord not healed him. It appears as the place of the dead, for righteous as well as wicked.

In 31:17 *Sheol* is the place to which the wicked go "dumbfounded" (RSV), when the Lord delivers the psalmist from his enemies (the wicked). Presumably these enemies are not preserved by the Lord, that is they are slain, and the psalmist is preserved alive. Sheol, then, is an undesirable fate, not so much because in itself it stands as God's judgment, but because it is the place of those who die.

Now, continue by studying the occurrences in Psalm 49:14,15; 55:16; 86:13; 88:3 (associated with "the grave"); 89:48; 116:3; and 141:7. Summarize your findings and draw conclusions about the meaning of the word *Sheol* as you have seen it used in the Psalms. If you wish to compare your findings with mine, check the footnote here.[13]

Based on this evidence, what would you say the psalmist meant in 139:8 by claiming that even if he "made his bed in Sheol," the Lord would be there? Remember that these few occurrences only give one a glimpse of what the psalmist meant when he used the word, *Sheol*. They do not provide sufficient information for developing a full-blown idea of the Bible's teaching on the afterlife, or hell, for example. To develop those views would require not only studying all the occurrences of this word, but of related terms as well. We would, in addition, take into account the

---

[13]In the Psalms *Sheol* seems to name the place of the dead, a place or realm from which persons desire to be delivered, or from which they testify to being delivered, by being saved from death. The eventual fate of all humans (88:48), it stands as the unenviable fate of the wicked as they enter it, having been slain or at least not delivered by the Lord.

development of ideas as they move through Scripture, so we would not expect the psalmist to give us all the information a New Testament believer might need.

4. In addition to this study of sample occurrences—or instead of doing our own study of the occurrences, if time did not permit—we could look up "Sheol" directly in a secondary source such as a Bible dictionary or one of the "word books" listed in the bibliography. Harris and Waltke's *Theological Wordbook of the Old Testament* has a four-column article on this word (vol. II, 892-893), which the English-only reader could locate through the index linking Strong's numbers with the *Wordbook* entries.

5. Moving to the clauses, "take the wings of the morning" and "settle at the farthest limits of the sea," in verses 8-9, we encounter terms where an unexpected set of ideas opens up to us. These ideas we would not have expected unless our familiarity with the ancient world reminded us that nearly all aspects of life were associated in some way or another with "the gods." Sea, earth, sun, moon, stars, storm, river, mountain are all among the gods, and for Israel's neighbors would be capitalized— Sea, Sun, Moon, and so on. All of these figured in the mythologies current in the psalmist's day. The God of Israel sought to lead persons to a knowledge of himself as the one, true, and living God, maker of all the things Israel's neighbors worshipped as gods (cf. Gen. 1; Is. 44; Ps. 19). But even in Israel, persons lived constantly in contact with culture that assumed "the gods" and the world view associated with them.

In the case of "morning," a word study will yield little, because the key to its significance lies in background information. Noting that the NAB translates this "the wings of the dawn," if we look up "dawn" in a multi-volume Bible dictionary, like *The Anchor Bible Dictionary* (vol. II, 72), we will be led to "Shahar," (vol. V, 1150-

1151), who was the Dawn, twin offspring with Dusk of the High God, El. Turning to the entry for the "Sea" (vol. V, 1058-1059), we locate similar evidence about "Prince Sea" in the psalmist's world.

This information leads us to the conclusion that in these clauses the psalmist has more in mind than simply going as far as possible to the East or to the West, although this idea of great distance is no doubt involved. Beyond the sheer range of the Lord's knowing presence in these unimaginably distant places, these are the realms of alien gods, territory quite likely held in awe, perhaps fear (certainly as far as the Sea goes), by the ancients.

So it seems likely that these affirmations about the Lord's presence in Sheol and the reaches of Dawn and Sea register powerful claims. In the most distant, foreboding, frightful, and awesome "places" of life or death imaginable, God is present. But that is not all. Looking further we note that in these "off limits" realms God is *actively, sovereignly* present, holding, leading, saving the psalmist (v. 10). Do you see the evidence for that?

6. These samples have illustrated the fact that different words in the text present different challenges and yield to different approaches. For some, our own word study will prove useful. For others, we may want or need to turn to a secondary source for help. Continue this sort of study as long as you are able, beginning at key words or difficult lines.

7. *Other interpreters.* Having done your own homework on this psalm, you will be able to understand and appreciate more adequately what others may say about it. If you have access to a commentary on the psalms, read its treatment of Psalm 139 now. How does it enrich your understanding? Which of your findings seem confirmed by the additional evidence found here? Which called into question? Summarize.

8. What significance do these findings have for you and the world you live in?

Let Jesus Be the Judge

1. You may find it helpful to review chapter 5.
2. At this point we assume you have come to at least pre-liminary conclusions about what you think Psalm 139 means—that is, what the psalmist meant as he prayed, and what contemporary readers of the psalm would have understood. As we anticipate asking what this prayer may have to do with our life and world, we must first listen to the rest of God's Word regarding the psalm's major ideas.
3. A summary of your understandings after study might well run along these lines:

   a. The psalmist believes the Lord God knows everything there is to know about him, a knowledge beyond his comprehension. God not only knows all about him, but actively oversees his life. Furthermore no place in which the psalmist might find himself, no matter how fearful or alien or distant, lies outside of God's active, knowing, leading presence. And no condition obscures or confuses his discernment of the psalmist's thoughts and deeds.

   b. The psalmist attributes this amazing knowledge at least in part to the fact that God created him. Using imagery of weaving and tapestries, he claims God knows him because he made him. And, wonder of wonders, the Creator remains thoughtfully, intensely interested, not simply in "creation" in general but in this creature of his.

   c. The psalmist responds to his prayerful reflection on these affirmations by declaring his disdain for the enemies of God and, by implication, siding with God, openly and without reservation. In this declaration of loyalty to God, he asks God to destroy these persons who are both God's enemies and his as well, apparently harassing him. It is entirely possible, as a matter of fact, that the accusations of these enemies have actually prompted this prayer. If so, then the preceding claims about God's amazing knowledge are both a comfort to him and intended as something of a vindication of him before God in the face of these accusations.

d. The psalmist concludes, then, by asking God to do what the entire song has claimed God does anyway—to "search" and "know" him. This constitutes a surrender, one might say, to the sovereign knowing of God, and a challenge in the face of his accusers. Beyond that, he would be led on in the way pleasing to God. Presumably, should God find fault in him, this stance implies the prayer that God not destroy him as one of the wicked, but restore and lead him as one eager to do the will of God.

5. What do we conclude if we listen to the rest of Scripture regarding these major statements of faith and petition? To illustrate the different sort of "conversation" one hears in Scripture, we will work with items a and b together and then c, the psalmist's faith regarding God's knowing as Creator and his prayer regarding the enemies of God. Of course, in the space we have here, we will just begin the process, but we can see how such an inquiry could go.

6. God's knowing as Creator. What other major passages of Scripture deal with God's knowledge of his creatures, particularly of human beings? How would we locate such passages beyond those we may already know.

a. *Concordance.* An English language concordance could lead us to passages which use the words translated "know," some of which would no doubt speak of God's knowing. This would at least be a place to start. (Note: as always, we will look at each reference *in its context*, to catch its sense in its setting and, if possible, the point of the passage involved.) The following texts speak of God's or the Lord's knowing: Genesis 3:5, 22; 15:13; 20:6; Exodus 3:7; 4:14; 32:22; 33:5, 17; Deuteronomy 3:19; 8:2; 13:3; 31:21; Joshua 22:22; Judges 3:4; 2 Samuel 7:20; *1 Kings 8:39* (cf. 2 Chron. 6:30); *2 Kings 19:27* (cf. Isa. 37:28); 2 Chronicles 32:31; Job 10:7; 31:6; Psalm 40:9; 50:11; 69:5; *73:11*; *94:11*; Proverbs 24:12; Isaiah 41:21-24; 66:18; Jeremiah 12:3; 15:15; 17:4, 16; 29:11, 23; 48:30; Ezekiel 11:5; Hosea 13:5; Amos 5:12; Matthew 25:12; Luke 13:25, 27; *Acts 1:24*; 1 Corinthians 13:12. These speak of Jesus' knowing or Christ's knowing: John 5:42; 7:29, 51; 8:55; 10:14-15; 13:18; *21:17*; Revelation 2:2, 9, 13, 19; 3:1, 8, 15. References in italics flag references of particular interest when read in light of Psalm 139.

Reviewing these texts in their contexts, what do you discover about God's knowing? How do these texts or their contexts relate God's role as Creator to his knowing? How do the claims or assumptions of these texts relate to those of Psalm 139? Do they affirm, revise, refute, expound, extend, or redirect? Summarize your findings.

b. *Cross-references for Psalm 139:1-18.* The cross-references provided in study Bibles might well lead to passages related topically to the one we have interpreted and provide a place to start. Consulting three study Bibles that provide cross-references for the NIV, the NKJV, and the NRSV, one finds that all three cited the following texts as worthy of consideration along with Psalm 139:1-18: 2 Kings 19:27; Job 31:4; 34:22; Psalm 17:3; 40:5; Jeremiah 12:3; 23:24; Daniel 2:22; Amos 9:2-3; Romans 11:2-3; Hebrews 4:13. Perhaps these would be the place to start, if one must limit the search. Two of the three also cited Job 10:11; 26:6; 42:3; Psalm 23:3; 34:7; 119:73; Proverbs 15:11; Eccelesiastes 11:5; Jonah 1:3; Matthew 9:4. Other texts cited by only one of the study Bibles were: Deuteronomy 30:12-15; 1 Samuel 25:16; Job 5:9; 9:33; 10:8-9; 14:16; 22:13; 27:3; 29:18; 33:29-30; 34:22; Psalm 3:5; 23:2; 32:10; 44:21; 63:9; 90:12; 92:5; 94:11; 108:6; 119:115; 125:2; 131:1; Proverbs 24:12; Isaiah 11:4; 41:10; 44:2, 24; 46:3; 49:5; 66:18; Amos 9:4; John 2:24.

Among these references one will find texts which relate only superficially or by word or phrase similarity to our text. Other references will lead to passages bearing significant relationship to the issues treated by Psalm 139.

Reviewing these texts in their contexts, assess them as you did those passages located by concordance (6.a above). Now summarize your findings regarding the cross-cultural claims and ideas about God's knowing.

7. Prayer for the destruction of God's enemies who are also the psalmist's enemies.

a. *Concordance.* The words "hate" (in its various forms, e.g., "hates," "hated") and "enemy," "enemies" from Psalm 139 should lead to relevant passages. The following occurrences speak either of God's hatred or of his people's hatred toward his enemies or theirs. Even though this is not a complete list from a concordance search of these words, it will provide a good start at discerning dominant approaches to these matters in Scripture. Genesis 22:17; Exodus 20:5; 23:22; Leviticus 19:17; Numbers 10:35; Deuteronomy 5:9; 6:19; 7:10, 15; 19:11; 23:14; 32:41; 33:11; 2 Samuel 22:1, 41(cf. Psalm 18:1, 40); 2 Chronicles 19:2; Esther 9:1; Job 31:29-30; Psalm 5:5; 6:8-10; 17:7; 21:8; 31:6, 11, 15; 34:19-22; 37:20; 38:17-22; 41:5-10; 54:1-5; 68:1-2, 21-23; 69:4, 14; 72:9; 83:1-2; 89:23; 97:3, 10; 108:13; 118:7; 119:113-120; 129:5; Proverbs 24:17; 25:21; Isaiah 1:24; 59:18; 66:6, 14; Nahum 1:2, 8; Matthew 5:43-44; 10:22; 24:9; Luke 1:71; 6:22, 27, 35; John 15:18;

Romans 5:10; 12:20; 1 Corinthians 15:25; Philippians 3:18; Hebrews 1:9; Revelation 2:6. (See the reflection questions below.)

b. *Cross-references for Psalm 139:19-22.* The same three study Bibles (for NKJV, NIV, NRSV) consulted above show no references cited by all three. Two of the three refer us to Psalm 119:115 (another to 119:113); Isaiah 11:4; 2 Chronicles 19:2 and Jude 15. Other references, cited by only one of the study Bibles were: Deuteronomy 5:11; Psalm 5:6; 6:8; 13:6; 26:5; 59:2; 65:7; 119:113, 158; and Matthew 5:43. Remember to examine these occurrences and those from the concordance *in context.*

Reflection questions for concordance and cross-reference search. What varying perspectives do you see from which these texts address the issue of hatred of the enemy? What distinctions seem important to make in considering these texts and their relevance to the prayer of Psalm 139? Do you see any change in approach as you move through Israel's history, as represented in these passages? What differences do you perceive between the approach of the Old and the New Testament in these passages? What similarities do you see between the New Testament texts cited and those examined from the Old Testament? In light of these similarities and differences and the canonical dialogue as you have discerned it to this point, in what ways do you think Psalm 139 speaks cross-culturally regarding one's attitude toward "the enemy"?

Clearly these questions and those issues raised by Psalm 139 are complex and far-reaching. We have a start, but just that. Hopefully we have examined enough evidence to caution us against dogmatic and over-confident claims, while motivating us to further study.

8. *Other interpreters.* Return, if possible, to the commentary you read in connection with your interpretive work. You were looking at that time for how the writer *understood* the psalm. Now see what indications the commentator has given regarding his or her conclusions regarding the enduring significance of the psalm for persons of other times and places. Reflect on what you find.

9. How do these findings revise or confirm or extend you previous notions as to the possible significance of Psalm 139 for you and your world?

Live the Word

1. You may find it helpful to review chapter 6, "Live the Word."

2. Using the "whole-life-application-probe," think about the various areas of human life touched by this psalm. Which seem most directly addressed? Which less directly?

3. We will use the "application questions" from chapter 6 to focus our thoughts. They might be adapted to Psalm 139, as we have studied it, something like this:

   a. In light of this prayer about God's amazing knowledge, and in light of the psalmist's response—his forceful siding with God and against those who hate God, and in light of my study of other scriptural teaching about these matters, what affirmations about God, Jesus of Nazareth, and myself should I make? What affirmations should I make about others and this world?

   b. In what ways does this prayer about the Creator's active and present knowing and about our response to that knowing confirm the good already present in my life and world?

   c. On the other hand, what sin should I confess, having studied this prayer and seen my Creator's knowing,

and having reviewed my own response to God's enemies and my own?

d. What changes should I make in my investment of
time, money, energy or other personal resources in
view of this prayer? What difference do the affirmations and confessions I have just recorded make for
these investments of mine?

e. What prayer of my own should I pray for myself and
my world, for my friends and particularly my enemies, in light of this psalm, as I have finally come to
understand it and its place in the canon?

Resources for Bible Study

Bible Study Method and Bible Interpretation

Fee, Gordon D. and Douglas Stuart. *How to Read the Bible for All It's Worth: A Guide to Understanding the Bible.* Grand Rapids: Zondervan, 1982.

Jensen, Irving L. *Independent Bible Study.* Chicago: Moody Press, 1992.

Mickelsen, A. Berkeley and Alvera M. Mickelsen. *Understanding Scripture: How to Read and Study the Bible.* Rev. ed. Peabody, MA: Hendrickson, 1992.

*Osborne, Grant R. *The Hermeneutical Spiral: A Comprehensive Introduction to Biblical Interpretation.* Downers Grove, IL: InterVarsity Press, 1991.

*Traina, Robert A. *Methodical Bible Study.* New York: Ganas & Harris, 1952; reprint, Grand Rapids: Zondervan, 1985.

Bible Dictionaries and Encyclopedias

Achtemeier, Paul J., ed. *Harper's Bible Dictionary.* San Francisco: Harper & Row, 1985.

Bromiley, Geoffrey W., ed. *International Standard Bible Encyclopedia.* Rev. ed. 4 vols. Grand Rapids: Eerdmans, 1979-1988.

Buttrick, George Arthur, ed. *The Interpreter's Dictionary of the Bible.* 4 vols plus Supplementary Volume. Nashville: Abingdon, 1962, 1976.

Douglas, J.D., ed. *The New Bible Dictionary.* Rev. by Norman Hillyer. Wheaton, IL: Tyndale House, 1982.

Indicates more technical, extended works

Freedman, David Noel, ed. *The Anchor Bible Dictionary*. 6 vols. New York: Doubleday, 1992.

Tenny, Merrill C., ed. *The Zondervan Pictoral Encyclopedia of the Bible*. 5 vols. Grand Rapids: Zondervan, 1975.

Concordances

Goodrick, Edward W. and John R. Kohlenberger III, eds. *The NIV Exhaustive Concordance*. Grand Rapids: Zondervan, 1990. (NIV)

Kohlenberger, John R. III, Edward W. Goodrick, and James A. Swanson, eds. *The Greek-English Concordance of the New Testament*. Grand Rapids: Zondervan, 1993.

Strong, James. *The New Strong's Exhaustive Concordance of the Bible*. Reprint. Nashville: Thomas Nelson, 1990. (KJV)

Thomas, Robert L., ed. *The New American Standard Exhaustive Concordance of the Bible*. Nashville: Holman Bible Publishers, 1981. (NASB)

Wigram, George V. and Jay P. Green, Sr. *The New Englishman's Greek Concordance and Lexicon*. Peabody, MA: Hendrickson, 1992.

Wigram, George V. *The New Englishman's Hebrew Concordance*. Peabody, MA: Hendrickson, 1992.

Young, Robert. *Young's Analytical Concordance of the Bible*. Reprint. Peabody, MA: Hendrickson, 1984. (KJV)

Wordbooks

Brown, Collin, ed. *The New International Dictionary of New Testament Theology*. 3 vols. Grand Rapids: Zondervan, 1975-1979.

Harris, R. L.; G. L. Archer; and Bruce K. Waltke, eds. *Theological Dictionary of the Old Testament*. 2 vols. Chicago: Moody, 1980.

Commentaries, One Volume

Brown, Raymond E., Joseph A. Fitzmyer, and Roland E. Murphy. *The New Jerome Biblical Commentary*. Englewood Cliffs, NJ: Prentice-Hall, 1990.

Carpenter, Eugene and Wayne McCown, eds. *Asbury Bible Commentary*. Grand Rapids: Zondervan, 1992.

Elwell, Walter A., ed. *Evangelical Commentary on the Bible*. Grand Rapids: Baker, 1989.

Guthrie, Donald and James A. Motyer, eds. *The New Bible Commentary*. 3rd ed. London: InterVarsity, 1970.

Laymon, Charles M., ed. *The Interpreter's One-Volume Commentary on the Bible*. Nashville: Abingdon, 1971.

Mays, James Luther, ed. *Harper's Bible Commentary*. San Francisco: Harper & Row, 1988.

For multivolume commentaries consult the book lists below or ask at local book stores.

Historical Context of the Bible

Bright, John. *A History of Israel*. 3rd ed. Philadelphia: Westminster, 1981.

Bruce, F. F. *New Testament History*. Garden City, NY: Doubleday, 1972.

Harrison, R. K., ed. *Major Cities of the Biblical World*. New York: Nelson, 1985.

Pritchard, James B., ed. *The Harper Atlas of the Bible*. New York: Harper & Row, 1987.

Yamuchi, Edwin. *Harper's World of the New Testament*. San Francisco: Harper & Row, 1981.

Computer Software for Bible Study

*acCordance. The Gramcord Institute. Vancouver, WA (Mac)

AnyText. Linguist's Software. Edmonds, WA (DOS).

---

*Indicates more technical, scholarly level.

BibleSource. Zondervan. Grand Rapids, MI (DOS).

BibleWorks for Windows. Hermeneutika. Seattle, WA (DOS, Windows).

*GRAMCORD. The Gramcord Institute. Vancouver, WA (DOS).

Logos Bible Software. Logos Research Systems, Inc. Oak Harbor, WA (DOS, Windows).

MacBible. Zondervan. Grand Rapids, MI (Mac).

OnLine Bible. OnLine Bible USA. Bronson, MI (DOS).

WORDsearch for Windows. NavPress Software. Colorado Springs, CO (DOS, Windows).

Book Lists and Sources for Locating Other Resources

Bauer, David R., ed. *Biblical Resources for Ministry.* Asbury Theological Seminary: Division of Biblical Studies, 1989.

Childs, Brevard S. *Old Testament Books for Pastor and Teacher.* Westminster, 1977.

Christian Computing Magazine. Christian Computing Inc., Raymore, MO 64083.

Moo, Douglas, ed. *An Annotated Bibliography on the Bible and the Church.* Compiled for the Alumni Association of Trinity Evangelical Divinity School, 1986.

---

*Indicates more technical, scholarly level.